ANNUAL UPDATE **2018**

UK GOVERNMENT & POLITICS

Neil McNaughton
Eric Magee

HODDER
EDUCATION
AN HACHETTE UK COMPANY

Hodder Education, an Hachette UK company, Blenheim Court, George Street, Banbury, Oxfordshire OX16 5BH

Orders

Bookpoint Ltd, 130 Park Drive, Milton Park, Abingdon, Oxfordshire OX14 4SE
tel: 01235 827827
fax: 01235 400401
e-mail: education@bookpoint.co.uk

Lines are open 9.00 a.m.–5.00 p.m., Monday to Saturday, with a 24-hour message answering service. You can also order through the Hodder Education website: www.hoddereducation.co.uk

ISBN 978-1-5104-1507-2

First printed 2018

Impression number 5 4 3 2 1

Year 2021 2020 2019 2018

Typeset by Integra Software Services Pvt. Ltd., Pondicherry, India

Printed by CPI Group (UK) Ltd, Croydon, CR0 4YY

Hachette UK's policy is to use papers that are natural, renewable and recyclable products and made from wood grown in sustainable forests. The logging and manufacturing processes are expected to conform to the environmental regulations of the country of origin.

Contents

Contents

Chapter 1

The 2017 general election: an earthquake or just a tremor?

Exam success

The up-to-date facts, examples and arguments in this chapter will help you to produce good-quality answers in your AS and A-level tests in the following areas of the specifications:

Edexcel	AQA
1.3 Electoral systems	3.1.2.2 Elections and referendums
1.4 Voting behaviour and the media	

Context

Theresa May, the former home secretary, became prime minister in July 2016 following the resignation of David Cameron and her election as Conservative Party leader. She inherited a small parliamentary majority and there was widespread speculation that she would ask parliament for an early general election to give herself a mandate and increase her party's majority. However, Mrs May resisted this temptation and seemed set to carry on until the next scheduled election in 2020. It was, therefore, a major surprise when she announced, in April 2017, that she would seek parliamentary approval for a general election to be held on 8 June. Her reasoning was twofold:

- First — and this was the official explanation — she sought a large parliamentary majority so that she would have a strong mandate and unopposed backing for her government's Brexit negotiations, which were about to commence.
- The second reason was often described as 'opportunism'. The Labour Party was in disarray, as was UKIP, and there was no sign of a Liberal Democrat revival. A majority of over 100 was on the cards. The opinion polls were suggesting a possible landslide victory.

Events, however, turned out to be very different to all the predictions.

What happened to the Fixed-term Parliaments Act?

Before looking at the 2017 election itself, we should examine the circumstances whereby an early general election can be held. The Fixed-term Parliaments Act of 2011 had required that there be a fixed gap of 5 years between general elections (a system used by most modern democracies, though a 4-year gap is more common). Before the Act, the date of a general election was determined by the prime minister him- or herself. So how was it that Theresa May was able to call an election only 2 years after the previous poll?

The answer lies in the terms of the Act. It allows for two procedures whereby an early election can be held, namely:

- the passage of a vote of no confidence in the government in the House of Commons
- the approval of a two-thirds majority in the Commons

It was the second device that Mrs May chose and she was successful. Most of the Labour Party supported the motion to hold the election and so there was a large majority in favour.

We can, therefore, now confirm that the constitutional rule for early elections is that they can be called by the prime minister, but that he or she requires the approval of parliament, one way or another, to enforce the decision.

The nature of the 'earthquake'

By almost any standards, the 2017 general election was extraordinary in all its aspects — the nature of the campaign, the results and the aftermath. Below is a summary of the events:

- The campaign itself had a huge impact on the outcome. Campaigns are normally reckoned to have only a marginal effect on the result. At the start of this campaign, the Conservative Party was well ahead of Labour in the opinion polls. Some polls had the party over 20% ahead (which would have been converted into a parliamentary majority of close to 200). By the time of the election, the two main parties were almost neck and neck. In 6 weeks there had been a dramatic turnaround in their fortunes. The Conservative campaign proved to be as unsuccessful as Labour's was effective.
- No party won an overall majority, an outcome that has now occurred only three times since 1945.
- The Labour Party and its leader, Jeremy Corbyn, enjoyed an amazing and unexpected revival in their fortunes. At the start of the election campaign, both Corbyn and his party were widely seen as unelectable, but they came close to victory and have become favourites to win the next election.
- The Scottish National Party's complete domination of Scotland was brought to an end, as it lost many of its seats.
- UKIP's share of the national vote plummeted and the party ceased to be a significant factor in UK politics.
- For the first time in many years, a significant proportion of young voters turned out at the polling stations. Turnout among 18–24-years-olds had fallen to just over 40% at recent elections, but there was a major recovery in 2017.

The result in statistics

In order to evaluate the result of the 2017 general election, it is important to compare the result with that of the 2015 election. Table 1.1 illustrates the changes that took place in those 2 years.

Table 1.1 Seats won, 2015 and 2017

Party	Seats won 2015	Seats won 2017	Change
Conservative	330	317	−13
Labour	232	262	+30
Lib Dem	8	12	+ 4
SNP	56	35	−21
UKIP	1	0	−1

The Conservatives had an overall majority of 12 in 2015 but were nine seats short of an overall majority in 2017.

Table 1.2 Percentage of national vote won, 2015 and 2017

Party	% won 2015	% won 2017	Change
Conservative	36.9	42.3	+5.4
Labour	30.4	40.0	+9.6
Lib Dem	7.9	7.4	−0.5
SNP	4.7	3.0	−1.7
UKIP	12.6	1.8	−10.8

We can see that, in terms of numbers and statistics, the changes in the fortunes of the main parties that took place between 2015 and 2017 were not particularly dramatic. Indeed, the Conservatives, who were judged to have done extremely badly, increased their proportion of the national vote by 5.4% (Table 1.2). Table 1.1 also shows that the number of seats the Tories won fell by only 13. So why was this seen as such a catastrophe for the Conservatives? There are a number of reasons:

- At the start of the campaign the Conservatives were, according to most opinion polls, between 14 and 20% ahead of Labour in terms of national support. At the end the campaign they beat Labour by only 2.3% of the national vote.
- Having been on course for a majority of over 100, the Conservatives lost their parliamentary majority altogether.
- In the contest between the Conservatives and Labour, the latter made huge progress. Labour's share of the national poll rose by nearly 10%.
- The UKIP vote collapsed (see Table 1.2), from over 12% to less than 2%. It was expected that the Conservatives would and should pick up most of these defecting UKIP voters, but it was Labour that gained more of them, suggesting that it had made a stronger appeal to the less well off in UK society.

There was, however, one positive aspect for the Conservatives. In Scotland, the party increased the number of seats won from only one in 2015 to 12 in 2017, five more than Labour's representation there. This was largely the result of a successful campaign run by the Conservative Party leader in Scotland, Ruth Davidson.

The revival of support for Labour contained a number of key aspects:

- Foremost was the performance of the party leader, Jeremy Corbyn. Starting the campaign as a 'no-hoper', he grew in stature over the weeks before the election and caught up with Theresa May in popularity polls.
- Young people voted in much larger numbers (see Table 1.3), and these were largely Labour supporters.
- In areas where there had been a strong 'Remain' vote in the 2016 EU referendum Labour did especially well. The Conservatives were unseated in seats such as Twickenham and Battersea.

Table 1.3 shows the breakdown of voting for the parties by age in 2017, including the turnout among various age groups.

Table 1.3 Age and voting in 2017 (%)

Age range	Conservative	Labour	Lib Dem*	Turnout
18–24	18	67	7	54
25–34	22	58	9	55
35–44	30	50	9	56
45–54	40	39	9	66
55–64	47	33	9	71
65+	59	23	10	71

* Lib Dem voting is shown as higher than the actual vote owing to polling errors.

Sources: Ashcroft Polling/Ipsos MORI.

The breakdown of support for the various parties by age reveals how much there is a youth bias towards Labour and, conversely, that older voters predominantly support the Conservatives. The key fact here is that voting among the 18–24 age group jumped from about 40% in 2015 to 54% in 2017, hugely favouring Labour.

Professor John Curtice of Strathclyde University, probably the foremost election analyst in the UK, summarised the outcome of the election for the BBC (www.bbc.co.uk/news/election-2017-40219338) by identifying six key features:

1 The Conservatives did best in areas where there was a strong 'Leave' vote in the 2016 EU referendum, while Labour did especially well where 'Remain' voters had been most common. This meant that the swing towards the Conservatives or towards Labour was very uneven throughout the country.

2 The Conservatives lost considerable support among the middle classes (the majority of whom voted to remain in the EU) but gained working class votes (most of whom voted to leave). The opposite was true for Labour. This meant that the relationship between class and voting was weakened. See Table 1.4 below.

3 Jeremy Corbyn proved to have a very strong appeal among young voters. In areas where there was a preponderance of young voters (mostly students) Labour did especially well. Bristol, Canterbury and Cardiff were examples of large swings from Conservative to Labour.

4 The SNP did badly in Scotland, losing a third of its seats. This weakens the continuing case for Scottish independence. The Conservative Party was the main beneficiary of the SNP's decline.

5 The Liberal Democrats made virtually no progress, suggesting either weak leadership or the continuing legacy of their unpopular performance in the 2010–15 coalition.

6 UKIP was all but destroyed, losing its one seat and most of its electoral support.

In summary Curtice asserted that 'everybody lost'. He is right in the sense that no party got what it wanted (with the possible exception of the Democratic Unionist Party, which became a key partner with the Conservatives by holding the balance of power at Westminster). Labour could celebrate the most, but this cannot disguise the fact that the party has now lost three elections in a row.

Table 1.4 Social class and voting in 2017 compared with 2015

Social class	Conservative (%)		Labour (%)		Lib Dem (%)	
	2015	2017	2015	2017	2015	2017
AB	45	46	26	38	12	10
C1	41	41	29	43	8	8
C2	32	47	32	40	6	6
DE	27	41	41	44	5	5

Sources: YouGov (2017), House of Commons (2015).

Table 1.4 demonstrates clearly that social class was a much less reliable indicator of support for the main parties in 2017 than it had been in 2015. In 2017 voting for the two main parties was quite evenly spread across the social classes.

The aftermath of the election

A lame duck prime minister?

It may well be that, by the time you are reading this, Theresa May is no longer prime minister. That is a measure of the precariousness of her position. At the time of writing in autumn 2017, her position has been weakened in a number of ways:

- She has lost her parliamentary majority. This means she will have great difficulty steering through her legislative programme.
- She has lost authority by making an error of judgement in calling an unnecessary general election.
- She has also lost authority in that there is a general belief that she campaigned poorly in 2017.
- As the UK negotiates its departure from the EU, she has to balance the interests of her partner the DUP, the right-wing 'hard Brexiteers' in the Conservative Party and the 'soft Brexiteer' Tories. This may prove to be beyond her.

The main factor in her favour is that few members of the Conservative Party want to face another general election too soon. Her defeat would almost certainly precipitate a general election. There are strong indications that Labour might win such an election and, more seriously for the Tories, it would be led by Jeremy Corbyn, who would make an extremely left-wing prime minister.

What has the election done to the Brexit process?

Pessimists suggest that the existence of a minority government will make a rational Brexit process virtually impossible. The Conservative Party is divided, Labour and the Liberal Democrats are unlikely to cooperate, and there is no political consensus for how the UK is to conduct negotiations with the EU. Had the Conservative Party under Theresa May won a decisive majority, there would have been few problems. The Conservative leadership group would have developed a Brexit policy and could have enforced this in parliament. But this has not happened.

The election also confirmed what had been revealed in the 2016 referendum — that the country is divided on whether there should be a 'hard' Brexit (i.e. the UK would leave the Single Market and Customs Union and exercise full control over the movement of people and labour) or a 'soft' Brexit (probably with the UK staying in the Single Market and allowing free movement of people and labour).

The restoration of the two-party system?

In 2017 the two main parties won 82.3% of the total national vote. This represents a reversal of a trend that has been seen for many years — the steady decline of the dominance of the two parties. Table 1.5 demonstrates this change.

Table 1.5 National vote won by the Conservative and Labour parties (%), 1997–2017

Election year	Vote won by the two main parties (%)
1997	73.9
2001	72.4
2005	67.6
2010	65.1
2015	67.2
2017	82.3

If we look at the proportion of the vote won by the two main parties in England alone in 2017, the position is even more evident. The two parties secured 87.5% of the total vote.

Whether or not this is permanent largely depends on the fortunes of the Liberal Democrat Party. At just over 7% of the national vote, the Liberal Democrats scarcely figure in the electoral calculus, but if they can return to a proportion of the vote in double figures, they may begin to erode two-party dominance again. The prospects for UKIP making a comeback look even more bleak as the party is in disarray and its key objective — the UK leaving the EU — has been achieved.

Is there a revival of the political left?

The short answer to this is 'yes'. Labour, with a radical, left-wing manifesto, won 40% of the vote, the most it has won since 2001 when the party under Tony Blair was more moderate. Furthermore, the party's leader, Jeremy Corbyn, has enjoyed growing public esteem. If we scratch the surface, however, we find that this revival may prove to be fragile.

The majority of Labour MPs elected in 2017 are not Corbyn supporters. Even the shadow cabinet is not united, with deputy leader Tom Watson often finding himself at odds with his leader. It also has to be pointed out that, although there was a Labour resurgence in 2017, the party still lost and there is no reason to suppose it could win an overall majority in the next election. The key factor for the left would appear to be whether the increase in voter turnout among the younger age groups can be sustained or even increased.

Do the detailed election results suggest the UK is a more divided society than ever before?

If the UK was divided over the EU referendum, it was even more split in the 2017 general election. Put together, the EU referendum and the 2017 general election reveal schisms in UK society. Table 1.6 summarises the principal divisions.

Table 1.6 Political divisions in UK society

Division	Evidence
Young versus old	There is a huge division between the young supporting Labour and the older age groups voting Conservative. The vast majority of the young voted to remain in the EU; the opposite was true of older age groups.
Cities versus countryside	In most urban areas there was a majority for remaining in the EU and Labour did well in the cities. The opposite was true for rural areas.
Middle class versus working class	In the EU referendum the middle classes mostly voted to remain, while the working class typically voted to leave. However, class did have a reduced impact on voting in the election.
North versus South	Labour still dominates voting in northern England, while the South remains solidly Conservative.
Ethnic minorities versus white British	There were large majorities among members of ethnic minorities for remaining in the EU and for Labour. The white British population is more balanced.

Where does this leave the main parties?

Conservatives

The party is very divided, particularly over the terms of Brexit, but also over whether the government should continue with economic austerity or should pursue a more expansionist policy. Divisions are also emerging over Theresa May's leadership. Unity in the party is unlikely to return until the Brexit process is completed.

Labour

Labour is as divided as the Conservatives and the issues are similar – over Brexit and the leadership. Unity in Labour will be more difficult to achieve than for the Conservatives. This is because there are deep ideological divisions among Labour MPs and members. Prospects for a future election victory may unite the party, but this unity is likely to be superficial and temporary.

Liberal Democrats

The party lost its leader, Tim Farron, who resigned shortly after the election. His successor, Vince Cable, is widely respected but also tainted by broken promises during the last coalition government and is thought by some to be too old, at 74. With the revival of Labour on the centre-left, the prospects for the party do not look promising as it will be increasingly difficult for the Liberal Democrats to distinguish themselves from Labour.

Scottish National Party

The SNP remains dominant in Scotland, but it has lost its pivotal role in UK parliamentary politics. The main effect of its disappointing showing in the general election is that demands for Scottish independence have been all but abandoned.

UKIP

UKIP is in the worst position of all the parties. Like the Liberal Democrats it lost its leader after the election and has been experiencing great difficulty finding a successor. The party is haemorrhaging members and it is losing seats in local government. Above all, however, it has been marginalised in the Brexit process. Its one hope is that its former leader, Nigel Farage, will re-emerge to arrest its decline.

Conclusion

The title of this chapter asks whether 2017 was an earthquake or just a tremor. If we pursue the metaphor we must ask whether the tectonic plates of politics in the UK have indeed shifted, representing an earthquake. The evidence that there has been a fundamental change includes the following features:

- The decline of the Liberal Democrats and the poor performance of UKIP and the Green Party does suggest a reversion to a two-party system.
- The strong link between social class and voting behaviour seems to have been weakened.
- There is now a strong difference in party support between urban and rural areas, with Labour strong in large towns and cities and the Conservatives established in rural and suburban areas.
- If turnout among the young remains high, and possibly increases, there will be a revival of left-wing politics in the UK.

On the other hand, it may well be that the changes described here are temporary. In some senses there has been only temporary or modest change, in other words a tremor rather than an earthquake:

- Scotland, Wales and Northern Ireland remain multi-party systems.
- England is still a two-party system as it always has been. Labour and the Conservatives won the vast majority of the national votes.
- With the declining importance of small parties, the UK should return to single-party majority government in the future.

Exam focus

To consolidate your knowledge of this chapter, answer the following questions:

1 What were the main features of the outcome of the general election of June 2017?
2 Account for the revival of the Labour Party's electoral fortunes in 2017.
3 Assess the role of opinion polls in the 2017 general election.
4 Assess the importance of regional variations in voting patterns in 2017.
5 Are the divisions *within* the main parties more significant than the differences *between* them?

Chapter 2

After the 2017 general election: governing without a majority

Exam success

The up-to-date facts, examples and arguments in this chapter will help you to produce good-quality answers in your AS and A-level tests in the following areas of the specifications:

Edexcel	AQA
1.3 Electoral systems	3.1.2.2 Elections and referendums
2.3 Prime minister and executive	
2.4 Relations between institutions	

Context

The last time a general election failed to return an overall parliamentary majority was in 2010. On that occasion a coalition government was formed between the Conservative Party and the Liberal Democrats. The coalition had three main features:

1 Ministerial posts were shared between the two parties.
2 There was an agreed political programme between the two parties.
3 When parliament was considering agreed policies, it was expected that the two parties would work together to ensure a parliamentary majority for the measures.

It was immediately clear in 2017, however, that such a formal arrangement was impossible. The Liberal Democrats were too far apart from the Conservatives (especially over Europe and Brexit) to consider another coalition. The same was true of the Scottish National Party, and none of the other small parties was large enough or politically close enough to the Conservatives. A 'grand coalition' between the Conservatives and Labour was out of the question, not least because Labour had adopted a radical, left-wing set of policies under Jeremy Corbyn's leadership. This left only two alternatives — a second election in the hope of resolving the deadlock, or a minority government. Mrs May and her colleagues, as the largest party, were granted the first choice and decided to struggle on. However, they were offered a lifeline by the small Democratic Unionist Party (DUP) in Northern Ireland.

Confidence and supply

These two terms have become important in relation to the survival of the minority government that took office in June 2017.

Confidence

'Confidence' refers to the issue of whether parliament (in particular the House of Commons) has confidence in the government to govern effectively. If parliament passes a vote of no confidence in the government it is effectively dismissing that government. If that occurs, either another party must become the government or there must be a general election.

It therefore follows that a government that loses a vote of confidence cannot govern. If a government does not command a majority in the House of Commons, then as soon as a controversial policy is proposed it will lose the vote and probably be dismissed. It will, in short, not survive for long.

Supply

'Supply' is an ancient parliamentary term referring to the granting of authority to the government (in past times, effectively the monarch) by parliament for raising taxes and spending the revenue. Supply meant the supply of tax and other revenues for public expenditure. If parliament refuses to grant this authority, the government is paralysed and cannot continue. In effect this entails a vote against the government's budget proposals.

When Theresa May decided to form a minority government after the 2017 election she approached the small Northern Ireland Democratic Unionist Party (DUP) with a 'supply and confidence' proposal. This was an agreement that the DUP would support the government in a supply vote or in a vote of no confidence. The party held eight seats in the Commons, enough to give the Conservatives an overall majority. In return for this agreement, the government committed an additional grant of £1 billion for various projects in Northern Ireland.

This agreement does *not* mean that the DUP will support the Conservative government on *all* issues, but only on matters of supply and confidence. In this way the government is able to survive, for the time being at least.

Who and what is the DUP?

The unionist movement in Northern Ireland has existed since the province came into existence in 1921. Unionists strongly support the union of Northern Ireland and the rest of the UK. In other words, they are violently (literally, in the past) opposed to the nationalist, or republican, movement that seeks to introduce a united, independent Ireland.

Until 1971, at the beginning of the sectarian violence in Northern Ireland which was to last until the mid-1990s, the unionist movement was represented by the Unionist Party (UP). In that year, however, the party split and the Protestant leader, the Reverend Ian Paisley, founded the Democratic Unionist Party (DUP). The DUP was more conservative, more religiously based and more radically loyal to the UK than the Ulster Unionist Party (UUP), formed by the other unionists who did not support Paisley.

The main features of the DUP are:

- Its members are virtually all militant Protestants (known as Free Presbyterians) and therefore anti-Catholic.
- Their brand of Christianity is very conservative. They oppose abortion, tolerance of homosexuality and same-sex marriage.
- Members are fierce British patriots and are strongly pro-monarchy.
- It has usually opposed concessions to Irish nationalist, Catholic parties in the interests of peace in the province.
- Its general political stance is conservative and its members have normally voted with the UK Conservative Party in parliament.

Since its foundation in 1971 the DUP has gradually grown in support and eventually became the largest party in Northern Ireland. In 2017 it increased its representation at Westminster to eight. Its leader, since 2015, has been Arlene Foster.

The nature of minority government

In many European states, most of which operate proportional representation systems, coalition government is the norm. Minority governing is rare. In the UK, however, we are used to minority government in both Scotland and Wales.

In Wales Labour has twice governed — from 2003 to 2007 and from 2011 to 2016 — with no majority, though in these two cases the party held exactly half the seats in the assembly. Since 2016, Wales has been governed by a minority Labour government. In Scotland the SNP formed minority governments after the 2007 and 2016 parliamentary elections. These governments proved to be remarkably stable and so far they have seen out their full terms. The question is: how is it possible to govern without a majority? The answer is that a number of conditions have to be met:

- Fixed-term elections help as it is more difficult to unseat a government within a fixed-term system.
- In the case of the UK government after 2017, a confidence and supply agreement helped to provide some sort of stability.
- The government must avoid controversial issues. Thus, the Conservative government after 2017 immediately dropped contentious proposals to introduce more selective grammar schools and to reform the system of funding social care.
- The government needs to control the public bill committees in the House of Commons. These committees examine legislation and may propose amendments. Some amendments can effectively 'wreck' a piece of legislation so it is vital that the government should avoid important defeats in committee. Normally, when the government enjoys an overall Commons majority, it is also granted a majority of the membership of the committees. What happens with a minority government? Nobody knew until a motion in the Commons in September 2017 was passed that established the principle that, even though

it was in a minority, the government would enjoy a majority on the public bill committees. This was an apparently obscure, but nevertheless vital, event.

- The government must try to avoid major public internal rifts and, probably, unwanted leadership contests.

Can the government survive?

The early signs are good for the government. Several events give rise to this conclusion:

- As we have seen above, the government is set to control the public bill committees. By a majority of 19 it won a Commons vote on the issue.
- In the first big vote in the Commons, the government enjoyed a comfortable majority of 36 for its EU (Withdrawal) Bill (the so-called 'Brexit' or 'EU Divorce' Bill). Every Conservative MP supported the bill and a number of Labour MPs abstained.
- Most senior members of the Conservative Party recognise that the alternative to staying unified and supporting the prime minister is the probability of a general election and the strong possibility that Labour would win such an election. When there was a crisis over May's leadership in the autumn of 2017 all senior ministers rallied round the prime minister, so the party seems determined to cling on to power.

Despite these positive events, however, there are still dangerous waters ahead for the government. The principal potential problems include:

- Should there be a major schism and leadership challenge in the Conservative Party in the future, resulting in the fall from power of the prime minister, the government may lose its grip on parliament and another election will have to be held.
- If the Brexit talks go badly and possibly even break down altogether, the government may be forced to put itself in the hands of the electorate for a fresh mandate.
- If the Brexit talks do not satisfy the DUP, that party might withdraw its parliamentary support for the government, rendering it vulnerable to defeat.

How the Conservatives propose to govern without a majority

The most important way in which a minority government can survive is by only introducing policies for which there is a consensus of support and avoiding issues that are politically divisive. In the autumn of 2017 the Conservative government seemed to have recognised this requirement. At the party's annual conference, Prime Minister May announced a number of initiatives but avoided the potential problems. Table 2.1 describes some of the consensus policies and contentious issues faced by the government:

Table 2.1 Consensus and adversarial issues, autumn 2017

Consensus policies to be pursued by the government	Contentious issues abandoned or postponed by the government
It is proposed to introduce a cap on rises in energy prices. This is also Labour, Liberal Democrat and SNP policy.	The introduction of more selective grammar schools in England. The Conservatives would have struggled to persuade a majority to support this through both the Commons and the Lords.
Financing for up to 3 million apprenticeship places was proposed. Few politicians would oppose this, although the details might be contentious.	Changes to the way in which social care is to be funded. There was widespread parliamentary opposition to the plans.
A freeze on any increases in university tuition fees is to be implemented. This may still be problematic as Labour would wish to go further and reduce fees, but the party might support a freeze.	The Chancellor of the Exchequer abandoned a pledge not to raise income tax, National Insurance or VAT. Labour might support tax increases if the revenue is used to improve public services.
A large increase in government expenditure on house building was announced. Here again, other parties might wish to go further but would not oppose a modest rise.	A plan to remove the winter fuel allowance from better-off pensioners was cancelled. Many backbench Conservatives would not have supported this plan.

The key problem for the government remains, however, that there is no consensus on the bargaining position of the UK with regard to Brexit. There is, therefore, no guarantee that any agreement will receive parliamentary approval. The lack of consensus and a parliamentary majority certainly undermines the government's authority in its negotiations with the EU. This problem appears, at the moment, to be insoluble.

How might the government fall?

There are a number of scenarios which could spell the end of the government's life. These are the possible circumstances:

- The government (i.e. the prime minister) could decide that it cannot continue, or does not wish to do so, and will seek to hold a general election. This might occur, for example, if the government's budget proposals were rejected or if it lost a vote on a major piece of legislation. This is effectively what happened in the spring of 2017. In order to hold an election the government needs the approval of a two-thirds majority of the House of Commons. In order to achieve such a majority, the Labour Party would have to support the resolution.
- If the Conservative Party held a leadership election and Mrs May either did not stand or lost the election, the new leader might seek a general election in order to try to win a fresh mandate from the electorate.

- The government could simply resign without seeking a general election. In such circumstances the prime minister would inform the queen that she was resigning. In this case there is a possibility that the Labour Party might try to form a government. This would also be a minority government and would be unlikely to last very long, but it could endure long enough to set out a legislative programme.
- The government might lose a vote of no confidence in the House of Commons and thus be forced to resign. This might occur if the DUP, which currently supports the government, decided to withdraw that support for some reason. In such circumstances that Labour Party would introduce a confidence motion and the Conservative government would probably lose as it has no majority. A general election would follow such an occurrence.

At the end of 2017 none of these scenarios seems imminent, but it is generally agreed that it will be difficult for the government to survive until the next general election, scheduled for 2022.

Conclusion

The UK is very much in uncharted political waters. The last minority government — Labour from February 1974 to October 1974 — was short-lived and achieved very little. 2017 is very different. In particular the government is wrestling with the problem of how to negotiate a Brexit agreement that needs to achieve a consensus of support. The Labour government of 1974 faced no such critical situation. It was also true in 1974 that Labour expected to win a second election in a short time (it did win the general election of October 1974, albeit with a tiny majority). If there were an election in 2018, most commentators, as well as many Conservative politicians, strongly believe that Labour would win. For this reason there are many who would support the government trying to carry on for as long as possible.

A second problem faced by the government is that the governing party is itself internally split. This makes it especially difficult to establish policies that will enjoy a consensus of support. Some, indeed, believe the problems are so great that this can be described as a 'zombie' government. This may be an exaggeration, but it will be a difficult period. The most likely outcome would seem to be that the government will try to hang on at least until the Brexit negotiations are complete.

Exam focus

To consolidate your knowledge of this chapter, answer the following questions:

1 Why did the Conservatives fail to win an overall majority at the 2017 general election?
2 How are minority governments able to survive?
3 Distinguish between minority government, coalition government and majority government.
4 To what extent is the Conservative Party now 'terminally divided'?
5 Assess the current state of the centre-left in UK politics.

Chapter 3

City and regional mayors: how much power do they really have?

Exam success

The up-to-date facts, examples and arguments in this chapter will help you to produce good-quality answers in your AS and A-level tests in the following areas of the specifications:

Edexcel	AQA
2.1 The constitution	3.1.1.1 The nature and sources of the constitution
2.4 Relations between institutions	3.1.1.5 Devolution

Context

Although there are a large number of mayoralties in England and Wales, this chapter will concentrate on eight regions that have elected mayors with considerable powers. Table 3.1 shows the details of these city and regional mayors.

Table 3.1 Eight city and regional mayoralties

City or region	Mayor	Mayor's party	When established
London	Sadiq Khan	Labour	2000
Cambridgeshire and Peterborough	James Palmer	Conservative	2017
Greater Manchester	Andy Burnham	Labour	2017
Liverpool City Region	Steve Rotherham	Labour	2017
Tees Valley	Ben Houchen	Conservative	2017
West of England	Tim Bowles	Conservative	2017
West Midlands	Andy Street	Conservative	2017
Sheffield City Region	Vacant	–	Due 2018

Unfortunately, it is not possible to generalise about how much power these mayors have, as they vary from one locality to another. The powers of each mayor were negotiated with the government individually. We must, therefore, treat them separately.

Why elect mayors?

In the past local mayors were appointed by local councils, and many still are. The position was viewed as an honour for councillors who had served for a long time. The first elected mayor was seen in London in 2000, after which little progress was made in extending the principle. This changed when the coalition government of 2010–15 agreed to hold referendums in various places to ask whether local populations would support the development. The advantages of a single, popularly elected mayor include the following:

- Local elections suffer from low turnouts so councils lack democratic legitimacy. It is hoped and assumed that the elected mayors will attract more support and so enjoy greater legitimacy.
- This factor will also make them more democratically accountable.
- They may create a sense of civic pride and provide a focus for local development.
- They can provide strategic, regional leadership, especially in areas such as London and Greater Manchester where there are a large number of local authorities.
- They can represent the interests of their city or region more effectively than central government.

The experience of London, now that it has had an elected mayor for almost two decades, may offer some indications of the future prospects for elected mayors. Table 3.2 indicates the positive and negative experiences of London having an elected mayor.

Table 3.2 An assessment of London having an elected mayor since 2000

Positive aspects	Negative aspects
London has become a genuinely global city and enjoyed considerable economic growth.	Turnout at mayoral elections has been low, in the range of 34–45%.
High-profile political figures have filled the office.	There remain pockets of deprivation in parts of London.
The incidence of crime in London has been falling.	There has been little progress on improving housing provision in London.
Tourism to London has increased.	The mayor has been unable to persuade central government to maintain policing and emergency services at pre-2010 levels.
There have been improvements in public transport and a reduction in private vehicular traffic.	Arguably, race relations in London are not improving.
The atmospheric environment of London has improved.	

The mixed picture presented in Table 3.2 suggests that it will be some time before we are able to assess the introduction of more elected mayors.

The powers of the mayors

London

It is no surprise that the mayor of London has more powers than any other elected mayor. At first sight the powers and responsibilities of the mayor look extensive and impressive. They include:

- large-scale planning and housing
- emergency services
- policing and crime policy
- economic development
- public transport
- arts and tourism

However, the degree to which the mayor actually *controls* policy in these areas varies a great deal, not least because the mayor's budget is limited. The mayor receives funds from a variety of sources, including 'precepts' from the London boroughs, central government grants and a share of business rates, a local tax charged on commercial premises. Most of the income is outside his/her control. In other words, the mayor basically gets what he/she is given.

Spending by the mayor in 2017–18 was divided as shown in Table 3.3.

Table 3.3 Mayor of London expenditure plans, 2017–18 (selected)

Service	Planned expenditure (£ billion)
Policing and crime	3.27
Fire and emergency services	0.43
Transport for London	6.98
Mayor's office expenses	1.00

Source: London mayor's office.

These figures do not tell the whole story. We must examine what specific powers the London mayor has over these services, as well as the limits to those powers. We should consider the following services: policing and crime; fire and emergency services; transport and planning; other projects and minor services.

Table 3.4 summarises the London mayor's powers and the limits to those powers.

Table 3.4 Mayor of London: powers and limitations

Service	Powers	Limitations
Policing and crime	The mayor: • sets priorities and plans for combatting crime • sets the budget for policing • has a special crime-prevention fund • has influence over the appointment of senior London policy officers	• The mayor cannot change the laws being enforced by the police. • Powers of the police are controlled at central government level. • Funds for policing are limited. • The mayor does not actually appoint senior officers.

Service	Powers	Limitations
Fire and emergency services	• The mayor sets priorities.	• The mayor has no operational control. • Funds are limited.
Transport for London	• The mayor consults on public transport matters with Transport for London (TfL) and has great influence. He does have a budget available for public transport. • The mayor has overall control of traffic management such as the congestion charge.	• The mayor has no operational control of public transport. • Funds are relatively limited.
Planning	• The mayor is responsible for large-scale planning of roads and building developments.	• The mayor's rulings can be overruled by central government.
General	• The mayor has funds available for promoting tourism, community projects, the arts etc.	• The mayor's funds are relatively limited. Total income is limited by central regulations.

Manchester

Manchester is different to all the other cities and regions in that it now has control of its own budget for health and social care, currently standing at £6 billion. This places considerably more responsibility on the mayor, even though he/she does not directly control the health and social care services.

Unlike the London mayor, who is accountable to a separately elected Greater London Authority, the Manchester mayor is accountable to the 'Combined Authority', which includes representatives of the ten borough councils that make up Greater Manchester.

In other areas the Manchester mayor is less powerful than his/her London counterpart. Nonetheless he/she is an important figure and a key player in long-term plans to make Manchester into a 'Northern Powerhouse', as the former chancellor of the exchequer, George Osborne, described it. The Manchester mayor is to be consulted on the new HS2 rail link with London and Birmingham and on the development of new motorways across the north of England.

The main powers and limitations of the Manchester mayor are shown in Table 3.5.

Table 3.5 Manchester's mayor: powers and limitations

Service	Powers	Limitations
Policing and crime	• The mayor is in overall control, including how the budget is to be allocated to various uses. He/she also sets general policing and crime policy.	• The mayor works within a limited budget. • The police must operate within restrictions set by central government. • The mayor is accountable to the ten boroughs within Greater Manchester and could be overruled by them.

Service	Powers	Limitations
Fire and emergency services	• The mayor is in overall control, including how the budget is to be allocated to various uses.	• The same limitations apply as for the mayor's control over policing and crime.
Health and social care	• The mayor will have some influence over how the health and social care budget is allocated.	• The mayor is only one of 37 stakeholders (including the ten councils) who control the budget so his/her influence is very diluted.
Transport	• The mayor allocates the overall budget and has general responsibility for planning transport in the region.	• The mayor's planning must conform with the plans of the ten boroughs.
Housing	• The mayor has a budget for housing.	• The budget is limited and the mayor can be overruled by the ten borough councils.
Local economy	• The mayor has a small budget for economic and commercial development.	• This budget is very limited.
General	• The mayor has funds available for promoting tourism, community projects, the arts etc.	• The mayor's funds are relatively limited. Total income is limited by central budgeting.

The other city and regional mayors

As we have seen, it is impossible to generalise about the powers of the mayors outside London and Manchester, apart from the fact that these two mayors have more powers than all the others. In all cases the mayors have to cooperate with existing local authorities and are accountable to them. Table 3.6 outlines the typical powers, limitations and notable exceptions of other city and regional mayors.

Table 3.6 The powers, limitations and notable exceptions of elected mayors
(other than those in London and Manchester)

Typical powers	Limitations	Some notable exceptions
• Housing and planning • Transport • Education and skills • Economic investment	• Funding is limited. • The mayors cannot raise their own revenue. • Education only relates to post-16 and apprenticeship provision. • Planning decisions can be overturned by central government. • The mayors are accountable to the local authorities.	• The Liverpool mayor has more extensive powers over strategic planning for the whole Merseyside region. • The West Midlands (Birmingham) mayor has considerable extra responsibility for road transport in the region. • The Sheffield mayor and local authority will have greater responsibility for industrial development.

Are elected mayors an example of devolution?

Strictly speaking, the introduction of elected mayors with varying powers does not represent a further extension of the devolution process. This is for a number of reasons, including the following:

- Most of the powers represent a shift from one kind of local or regional authority to another. In other words, the powers of the mayors have not, on the whole, been transferred away from central government. In the case of devolution to Scotland, Wales and Northern Ireland, considerable powers *have* been devolved away from central government.
- The mayors do not have control of their own revenues in the form of taxation or borrowing. They have to rely on sources from local authorities or central government. If, in the future, mayors are given revenue-raising abilities, that would represent a major shift in power.
- The mayors have no responsibilities in relation to law-making. They have to accept laws and regulations set elsewhere, mostly by the UK parliament or by central government ministers.
- The overall powers of these mayors are relatively limited and are very much within the control of local authorities in their areas of jurisdiction. Devolved governments, on the other hand, have a great deal of control over the areas they govern and are rarely overruled by their elected parliament and assemblies.

The one exception to this analysis concerns Manchester. Here the responsibility for a large proportion of health and social care *has* been devolved away from central government. However, the elected mayor of Manchester has only some influence over this new health authority. As we have seen above, his/her influence is balanced against that of several other bodies.

The future prospects for elected mayors

There appears to be limited appetite for the creation of new elected mayors in other regions and indeed some regions recently voted *against* their introduction. There is a suspicion that they may be wasteful, add a further fiscal burden on government, and are an unnecessary additional layer of government. It is likely that central government and parliament will allow the creation of more elected mayors only if there is a clearly expressed local desire to see them. This is most likely to be channelled through local referendums.

A second question asks whether the existing mayors are likely to be granted additional powers in the future. While there may be some 'tinkering' with these powers, it seems unlikely that significant responsibilities will be transferred. Elected mayors will only become significantly more powerful if two developments occur. These are:

- being granted independent powers to raise money through taxation and borrowing
- being granted the ability, together with the authorities with whom they share power, to pass laws relating to their cities or regions (as in the USA)

Conclusion

The chapter title raises the question of how powerful the elected mayors are. The best answer is: probably not as powerful as may appear to be the case. Although, as we have seen, the powers of mayors vary, we can generalise about the limitations of their powers. In summary:

- They have a limited range of powers.
- In many cases their powers are shared with local authorities.
- In many cases their decisions can be overruled by central government or the UK parliament.
- Their funds are severely limited compared to those available to central government departments.
- They do not have power to raise their own revenues through taxation or borrowing.

Exam focus

To consolidate your knowledge of this chapter, answer the following questions:

1 What factors limit the powers of elected mayors in the UK?
2 What are the advantages of electing mayors?
3 Distinguish between the election of mayors and the devolution process.
4 What is meant by the term 'Northern Powerhouse'?
5 To what extent has the introduction of the London mayor been a success?

Robin Cook's resignation was more of an embarrassment to the government than an effective gesture. When Iain Duncan Smith resigned, however, it created a shock wave which ended with the government reversing its policy on disability benefits. Furthermore, when Duncan Smith returned to the backbenches he became a thorn in the government's side, especially his campaigning for the UK's exit from the EU.

Collective responsibility has come under pressure in recent times for a number of reasons:

- The coalition government in 2010–15 created a special problem as the government was staffed by members of two different parties with differing policies, in some cases policies which were diametrically opposed.
- Since 2015, governments have operated with a very thin parliamentary majority or no majority at all. This gives individual ministers much greater leverage against a fragile government. This potential leverage has proved to be too big a temptation for some ministers to pass up.
- The issue of whether the UK should leave the EU during the referendum campaign of 2016 proved to be so divisive, and so many Conservative ministers disagreed fundamentally on the issue, that collective responsibility had to be suspended to facilitate open debate.
- The growing importance of social media and its use by politicians has provided opportunities for ministers to express views that may be slightly at odds with government policy without causing a dramatic reaction.

It is important to distinguish between collective and individual ministerial responsibility. Individual ministerial responsibility refers to ministers who have made a serious error. This can be in their professional duties as a minister or can be the result of their personal conduct. Should the prime minister lose faith in a minister as a result of such occurrences, he/she may require the minister in question to resign. The minister may decide to resign before being dismissed.

Why collective responsibility is important

The importance of collective responsibility can scarcely be overemphasised. It has a number of functions:

- It creates a strong sense of unity within government, giving it strength and authority.
- It helps the prime minister to maintain authority by creating discipline within the governing elite.
- It enables ministers to disagree in private without jeopardising government unity.
- As it applies to *all* ministers it ensures that about 100 MPs will support the government in a parliamentary vote (the so-called 'payroll vote').

The fact that collective responsibility is so important means that when it is threatened the fortunes of the government will be extremely adversely affected.

Chapter 4

The central executive: what happened to collective responsibility?

Exam success

The up-to-date facts, examples and arguments in this chapter will help you to produce good-quality answers in your AS and A-level tests in the following areas of the specifications:

Edexcel	AQA
2.3 The prime minister and executive	3.1.1.3 The prime minister and cabinet

Context

Collective responsibility is a key convention of the UK constitution and an important feature of central governance. The principles of the convention, or doctrine, are these:

- The decisions agreed in cabinet are collective in nature and the whole government is collectively responsible for those decisions. This means that individual government members cannot disassociate themselves from a policy or decision.
- All members of the government, not just cabinet members but all ministers and their parliamentary aides, are expected to defend agreed government policies. This means that they are expected to support and promote those policies.
- The discussions held in cabinet are secret, allowing ministers to disagree and express personal views in the privacy of the cabinet room, in contrast to the requirement that they must toe the government line in public.
- If a minister disagrees with government policy, he/she is expected to resign from the government or remain silent about his/her disagreement.
- If a minister disagrees in public with a policy, he/she is likely to be dismissed by the prime minister.

The recent experience of collective responsibility

Resignations under the doctrine of collective responsibility are relatively rare, especially among members of cabinet. Two high-profile resignations in modern times have been these:

- **2003, foreign secretary Robin Cook** resigned from the Labour government in protest at Prime Minister Tony Blair's decision to support the American attack on Iraq in that year.
- **2016, work and pensions secretary Iain Duncan Smith** resigned over government proposals to cut the levels of benefits available to disabled people.

Collective responsibility and coalition government, 2010–15

It is a remarkable fact that, in the 5 years of coalition government, there were no major resignations from the cabinet under the doctrine of collective responsibility. Several ministers resigned under the doctrine of *individual* ministerial responsibility, but that is a completely different principle. How did this come about?

The answer lies in the arrangements that were put in place at the beginning of the coalition. In essence, policies were divided into two kinds. Where policies were the subject of fundamental disagreement between the Conservative and Liberal Democrat parties and it was impossible to resolve the differences, there was an 'agreement to differ'. Examples of agreements to differ included the decision to renew the UK's Trident nuclear submarine programme and some aspects of environmental policy including the proposed expansion of nuclear energy production. This meant that ministers from the two parties *could* disagree in public over such policy areas. Where the cabinet *did* reach an agreement on policy, ministers were obliged to adopt the principles of collective responsibility.

The result was a remarkably stable government despite the difficult circumstances. It should be added, however, that the Liberal Democrats suffered for their failure to challenge a wide range of policies, making them seem weak and ineffective. In the 2015 general election the party lost most of its parliamentary seats.

The EU referendum campaign

When, in February 2016, Prime Minister David Cameron announced that there would be a national referendum on the UK's membership of the European Union, an important problem immediately emerged. Senior members of the Conservative Party, including several ministers, did not accept the official government line, that the UK should remain a member of the EU. These ministers insisted they should have the right to campaign openly on the issue *without leaving the government*. Had Cameron insisted on retaining the doctrine of collective responsibility, the government would have been decimated.

It was therefore agreed that collective responsibility would be suspended on this particular issue. The decision solved the problem but did lead to claims that, if collective responsibility could be suspended on this issue, why not on other key policies? It also created a difficult situation after the referendum.

After the UK voted to leave the EU, the government was left with many ministers who were expected to carry out the wishes of the British people although they had openly disagreed with such an outcome. David Cameron himself resigned, but the rest of the cabinet did not follow suit. The divisions in the government revealed by the referendum campaign have carried on into the Brexit process; the government now appears weak and divided on this enormously vital issue.

Collective responsibility under pressure — Brexit and May's leadership

When the Conservative Party lost its parliamentary majority in the general election of June 2017 it became immediately apparent that the cabinet was coming under pressure to maintain its unity. A number of incidents have created the impression of fragility:

- The chancellor of the exchequer, Philip Hammond, broke ranks with the leadership by declaring that he believed there would be a lengthy transition period when the UK leaves the EU. This runs contrary to the proposal that the UK should simply leave the EU and all its strictures in March 2019. Hammond, who had been strongly in favour of remaining in the EU, declared himself as a 'soft Brexiteer' at a time when government policy seemed to be moving towards a 'hard Brexit'.

- In July 2017, foreign secretary Boris Johnson openly declared that he now opposed the government policy of holding down pay levels among public sector workers. Several other ministers, including environment secretary Michael Gove and health secretary Jeremy Hunt, indicated their support for Johnson. It seemed as though a full-scale cabinet revolt was in progress, possibly even a leadership challenge. In the event, this potential revolt fizzled out when the government agreed to relax the public sector pay cap.

- Also in July, Theresa May was forced to hold a special cabinet meeting at which she stressed the doctrine of collective responsibility, warning ministers that they faced dismissal if they were found to be leaking cabinet disagreements. Ironically, news of the warning was also leaked.

- As Brexit negotiations with the EU got under way, several ministers were 'briefing' (i.e. planting stories with the traditional or social media) different policy options concerning the UK's future relationship with Europe. In particular, in September 2017, Boris Johnson published an article proposing a different vision of post-Brexit Britain to that of the prime minister. Johnson was suggesting a very clean break from the Single Market and a low tax economy, while the government line is to pursue an agreement to remain in the market and to maintain a tight fiscal (taxation) policy.

- There remains widespread press speculation that senior ministers are planning a leadership challenge. However, when former minister Grant Shapps tried to mount a challenge in October 2017, senior ministers decided to rally round the prime minister. Collective responsibility was holding firm... but only just.

- In November 2017, Boris Johnson and Michael Gove appeared to challenge the government's Brexit negotiating position by insisting on a 'hard Brexit' in a private letter to the prime minister. This was widely interpreted as a covert leadership challenge.

Can Theresa May restore cabinet unity?

In the autumn of 2017 the prospects for Theresa May's leadership do not look promising. There have been many predictions that her demise is imminent. In August 2017 she asserted that she does not intend to succumb to her problems. Speaking during a visit to Japan she said:

> I'm in this for the long term. There's a real job to be done in the United Kingdom... It's about getting the Brexit deal right, it's about building that deep and special partnership with the EU, but it's also about building global Britain, trading around the world... I'm not a quitter.

Notwithstanding this show of defiance, however, she faces a number of problems:

- With no parliamentary majority she will have enormous difficulty getting any legislative proposals through parliament. This includes vital Brexit legislation.
- Having made the huge mistake of calling an unnecessary general election and then losing it, her authority and judgement have been called into question.
- Her cabinet is extremely divided, especially over Brexit. Her attempts to stifle open warfare have largely failed.
- She has several rivals who scarcely hide their ambition to succeed her. These rivals are also experienced ministers with considerable followings within the Conservative Party. These include Boris Johnson, Philip Hammond, Michael Gove and David Davis.
- Negotiations with the EU over the UK's exit have started poorly. A number of her critics have suggested that this is because she has failed to set a clear agenda.
- Perhaps most importantly, as we have seen, Mrs May has been unable to impose collective responsibility on her cabinet.

Conclusion

Despite the experience of coalition and minority government, nobody is calling for the permanent abolition of the convention of collective responsibility. This is because it is a linchpin of government. Without it the whole character of relations between the executive and parliament would change. A strong executive and a relatively weak parliament are essential features of the UK political system. Without the strength of collective responsibility, the executive, and the prime minister her- or himself, would be less able to dominate.

The current problems with collective responsibility may be the result of a 'perfect storm' of circumstances as we have described above. If 'normal service' is resumed in the future, i.e. a government with a decisive parliamentary majority, a prime minister in a dominant position and a more united governing party, collective responsibility is likely to be re-established.

Exam focus

To consolidate your knowledge of this chapter, answer the following questions:

1 Explain the operation of collective responsibility in government.
2 Explain why the doctrine of collective responsibility is so vital.
3 Distinguish between individual and collective ministerial responsibility.
4 How and to what extent has collective responsibility been threatened in the UK?
5 What problems does a prime minister face in controlling the cabinet?

Chapter 5

Pluralism: do social media enhance or threaten democracy?

Exam success

The up-to-date facts, examples and arguments in this chapter will help you to produce good-quality answers in your AS and A-level tests in the following areas of the specifications:

Edexcel	AQA
1.1 Democracy and participation	3.1.2.1 Democracy and participation

Context

During the last decade or so, the importance of the internet and the various social media, in terms of democratic politics, has grown exponentially. It could even be said that such politics has been completely transformed by these developments.

At first sight they represent an extension of democracy, an opportunity for people to engage in politics who would not normally become involved through the conventional channels of political parties and formal pressure groups. It is also increasingly true that younger people, who are notoriously apathetic about national politics, have become more politicised as they are more used to communicating and receiving information through social media. A closer investigation, however, can lead us to question this apparently obvious conclusion.

If we assume that democracy is always enhanced if pluralism is allowed to flourish, and if we also assume that pluralism is well served if people have a wide range of independent sources of information and opinion available to them, then we can look at social media positively. So far, so good. There is now a plethora of websites, campaign platforms, blogs and opportunities to express one's views. The problem, however, is that there is no guarantee that any of these sources of information is accurate. Furthermore, it is becoming increasingly difficult to distinguish between fact and opinion. We will review some of President Trump's famous tweets below, which we may find either amusing or alarming, but they demonstrate that he is expressing a fear that many share — the fear that media channels may not be giving us balanced and fair information.

This chapter will review the types of social media and internet activity that are available to those who may be interested in politics and political issues. It will also assess whether these developments do indeed enhance democracy or whether they may, in a variety of ways, actually threaten democratic society.

E-petitions

E-petitions have have become a common device by which campaign groups seek to put pressure on decision-makers. The government itself runs a site for such petitions and, if enough people sign a petition, parliament will often debate the issue. 38 Degrees and change.org are further examples of platforms carrying e-petitions. Table 5.1 describes some prominent examples from 2017.

Table 5.1 E-petitions with over 100,000 votes in 2017

Issue	Platform	Detail
Campaign to restore the right of Uber taxis to operate in London after its licence was revoked by Transport for London.	All major platforms	The licence was removed on the grounds of public safety. Millions of Londoners have come to rely on Uber taxis. Some oppose Uber as it adds so much to traffic congestion and, it is claimed, mistreats its drivers. About 850.000 people signed the e-petition.
Campaign to oppose the repeal of the Human Rights Act.	38 Degrees and the official government site	A petition held mainly to protect the rights of EU citizens in the UK.
Campaign to end the cap of 1% on public sector workers' pay increases.	38 Degrees	This is part of a wider political conflict. The government is in the process of relaxing the cap.
Campaign to end the EU imposition of VAT on tampons (the so-called 'tampon tax').	change.org	This tax was said to discriminate against women. It was successful and the tax has been removed.
Campaign organised by Nobel Peace Prize winner Malala Yousafzai to extend funding from the UN's *Global Partnership for Education* to pay for education for more girls globally to 12 years.	change.org	This is likely to be implemented. It was partly as a result of an earlier e-petition that Malala was awarded the Nobel Peace Prize.
A demand that there be a national referendum on the final terms of a Brexit deal.	Government site	This is being debated in parliament. Parliament has been granted a vote on the final deal.

At first sight e-petitions would seem to be an example of consultative democracy in its purest form. When we scratch the surface, however, we can find a number of problems. Table 5.2 compares the positive and negative aspects of e-petitions.

Table 5.2 E-petitions assessed

Positive aspects	Negative aspects
E-petitions are a pure form of democracy, expressing clear opinions, and they represent the balance of the weight of opinion.	In most cases there is no opportunity for people to express the opposing view.
They can be aimed at local and sectional issues which normally receive little attention.	There is no guarantee that people who sign a petition understand the issues. They may vote purely emotionally and accept the premise of the e-petition uncritically.
They can be organised at virtually no cost. This means campaign groups with limited funds may be able to make an impact.	It may be too easy for people to sign without giving an issue sufficient consideration.
They give opportunities for people to participate in political issues when they would not take part if a more active form of participation was required.	There may be fraud in the sense that some participants may sign a number of times and so distort the numbers.
Young people especially are used to taking part in online polls in a commercial setting, so political activity of this kind is more accessible to them.	The wording used in an e-petition may be misleading.
They can promote political debate outside the normal forums such as parliament.	Petitions, like referendums, reduce questions to a binary nature, a simple 'yes' or 'no', while most issues are actually more complex.

It would be a mistake to claim that the development of e-petitions has changed the political landscape significantly. It would also be simplistic to state that they enhance democracy, as we have seen above. Nevertheless, they may be serving to 'politicise' younger citizens and this may have a spill-over effect on voting and other forms of participation.

Twitter, Facebook and other platforms

Here we are considering the various means by which people can communicate with large numbers of other people quickly and in a very direct way. Concern is now growing that such media pose a serious challenge to democratic politics. Some have even warned that such media are a threat to democracy.

We set the scene by considering some of the more dramatic tweets sent out by Donald Trump during 2017. Though we may consider them with some amusement, we should remember that they come from the most powerful individual in the world and that they are read, often uncritically, by millions of people:

> Our country has been unsuccessfully dealing with North Korea for 25 years, giving billions of dollars & getting nothing. Policy didn't work! (9 Oct 2017)

Being nice to Rocket Man hasn't worked in 25 years, why would it work now? Clinton failed, Bush failed, and Obama failed. I won't fail. (1 Oct 2017)

Kim Jong Un of North Korea, who is obviously a madman who doesn't mind starving or killing his people, will be tested like never before! (22 Sep 2017)

We have made more progress in the last nine months against ISIS than the Obama Administration has made in 8 years. Must be proactive & nasty! (15 Sep 2017)

NBC news is #FakeNews and more dishonest than even CNN. They are a disgrace to good reporting. No wonder their news ratings are way down! (4 Oct 2017)

MAKE AMERICA GREAT AGAIN! (23 Aug 2017)

During the 2016 EU referendum campaign, social media clearly made a significant impact. To illustrate their importance, several examples can be quoted:

- #brexit enjoyed over 20 million views and 600 retweets per hour.
- #eu was seen by over 17 million viewers and was retweeted 117 times per hour.
- In April/May 2016, 5.4 million tweets were recorded on the subject of the referendum. Twice as many of these tweets expressed anti-EU views as those that were pro-Remain.
- A Twitter poll on 8 June 2016 predicted that Leave would win the referendum, a finding that gave a major boost to the Leave campaign.

Similarly, during the 2017 general election campaign, Theresa May suffered a challenging interview with Jeremy Paxman in May. This was followed by a 'storm' of Twitter messages which were negative towards Mrs May. Within a month the Conservative Party went from enjoying a large poll lead to failing to win a parliamentary majority.

Writing in the *Washington Post* on 9 October 2017, Pierre Omidyar identified six dangers posed by social media. These were as follows:

1 They have become echo chambers of opinion, reinforcing one-sided opinions and creating communities of like-minded people whose prejudices become exaggerated.

2 There is no safeguard against false information being propagated. Famously, this has been described as fake news. The users of such media do not have enough information to be able to distinguish fact from opinion.

3 Social media may create a false impression of how popular a person or a view actually is. The impressive numbers generated when social media messages trend are a one-sided snapshot of a temporary wave of opinion.

4 Social media can be manipulated by campaign organisations, individual political actors or parties to create a groundswell of opinion which is an illusion. With resources and organisation social media campaigns can be created without being grounded in any genuine expression of opinion.

5 Commercial methods, such as triangulation and algorithms, can be used to target particularly susceptible groups with political messages and so distort popular opinion.

6 It has become too easy to propagate messages containing anti-democratic material, such as intolerance, race hatred, religious bigotry and even incitement to violence.

All these problems create a challenge to democratic politics. Writing in *Newsweek* on 8 May 2016, Vyacheslav Polonski described a similarly pessimistic view:

> ...we're not ungovernable in the long term. However, our current political institutions are incapable of handling the dynamism and diversity of citizen opinions. They are susceptible to emotional bursts and intimidated by the power of internet users. The critical challenge is, therefore, to distinguish when a seemingly popular movement does actually represent the emerging general will of the majority and when it is merely the echo of a loud, but insignificant, minority.

Omidyar and Polonski were actually warning about the dangers of undemocratic populism. The point they make is not just that populism threatens democracy, but that social media have made it a much more potent force than it has been in the past.

Table 5.3 summarises the positive and negative impacts of social media on democracy.

Table 5.3 Social media and democracy — an assessment

Positive impacts	Negative impacts
Social media give widespread opportunities for people to participate in politics.	It is difficult to distinguish between truth and untruth or mere opinion.
They represent an 'open highway' for opinion to be disseminated.	They may allow undemocratic views to be disseminated.
They particularly help to politicise younger people, who have been notoriously apathetic about politics.	They may give the illusion of majority opinion which is not genuine.
They allow smaller groups with few resources to make their voices heard.	They may reduce complex issues to simple slogans and easy solutions.
They encourage single-issue politics.	It may be possible to manipulate social media to create illusions and to give the impression that some views are more widespread than they actually are.

Blogging

Blogging is the practice of publishing more measured and complex opinions and commentaries on the internet than those represented by 'instant' social media. Some prominent examples of blogs that are regularly viewed by tens of thousands of readers are shown in Table 5.4.

Table 5.4 Prominent examples of bloggers and their political stances

Blog name	General political stance
Guido Fawkes	Right wing
Iain Dale	Conservative
Left Foot Forward	Left wing
Conservative Home	Conservative
Nick Robinson	Non-aligned
Liberal Conspiracy	Centre-left
Huff Post	Non-aligned

In addition to these, all political parties and major campaign groups publish regular blogs. Blogs overcome many of the problems presented by more instant social media, but still have some drawbacks:

- They may present opinions as though they were facts.
- If their political stance is clear, they serve only to reinforce existing views and play little part in real political debate.
- They are relatively unregulated so there is no guarantee that the information they include is accurate. This was a particular problem during the EU referendum campaign, when many blogs quoted unproven statistics on both sides of the argument.

Having considered these problems, however, there is little doubt that blogs are a significant way in which political information can be spread to a discerning audience.

Conclusion

The importance of social media and the internet reached new heights in 2014–17, a period when there were two elections and two major referendums in the UK. How much influence they had is open to question, but there is strong evidence to suggest that they did have the following impacts:

- In the Scottish referendum, they encouraged large numbers of young people to take part, a feature that increased the 'yes to independence' vote as the young were considerably more pro-independence than other age groups.
- In the 2015 general election there was a major social media campaign warning people about the potential dangers of a Labour–SNP coalition. This may have encouraged some voters to shift their support to the Conservatives.
- In the EU referendum it is acknowledged that the 'Leave' campaign used social media more effectively than the 'Remain' camp.
- In the 2017 general election the Labour Party ran a massively successful social media campaign that succeeded in increasing turnout among the young and galvanised support for Jeremy Corbyn.

There seems to be no reason why the internet and social media won't continue to have a growing impact on democratic politics in 2018 and beyond.

Exam focus

To consolidate your knowledge of this chapter, answer the following questions:

1 Explain the role played by social media in modern politics.
2 To what extent can social media be said to be undemocratic?
3 How have social media affected the way in which pressure groups now operate in the UK?
4 Examine the arguments for and against the use of e-petitions.
5 Examine the link between social media and the rise of left-wing politics in the UK.

Chapter 6

The Supreme Court: is it too powerful?

Exam success

The up-to-date facts, examples and arguments in this chapter will help you to produce good-quality answers in your AS and A-level tests in the following areas of the specifications:

Edexcel	AQA
2.4 Relations between institutions	3.1.1.4 The judiciary

Context

During 2017 a number of cases were heard in the Supreme Court that gave rise to concerns that the court had become too powerful and was beginning to threaten the authority of the elected government and parliament. This chapter examines whether the experiences of 2017 can justify these fears.

The Supreme Court was set up in 2005 under the terms of the Constitutional Reform Act. It began operations in 2009. The court replaced the old 'judicial committee' of the House of Lords, which comprised the 12 most senior judges in the UK. In terms of its members, the Supreme Court was unchanged from the House of Lords committee. Its powers also remained unchanged although there was a new, non-political method established for appointing new judges when a vacancy arose.

Although the functions and powers of the court remained unchanged, there is little doubt that its authority was enhanced after the 2005 Act. This has resulted in it becoming increasingly active and independent. Its role was considerably enhanced by the 1998 Human Rights Act, which had already come into force in 2000. The existence of a codified set of rights (the European Convention on Human Rights (ECHR)) gave the court an additional resource with which to safeguard citizens' rights and control the power of executive government.

Although there are 12 members, the court usually sits with a smaller number presiding. Decisions are based on a simple majority of the judges. The court is led by a president. Baroness Hale became its president in October 2017.

The functions and powers of the Supreme Court

The Supreme Court is an appeal court. This means that the cases it hears have already been resolved in a lower court, usually the High Court. The losing side in such cases may appeal to the Supreme Court for a final, binding verdict. The court agrees to hear appeals where it feels that there is a broad principle at stake or where the issue is of great importance and may have wide implications. Its main functions are the following:

- Determining whether citizens' rights have been ignored or distorted by a decision made by a public body. The rights it seeks to protect may be contained in the ECHR, parliamentary statutes, common law, equity or European Union legislation (the latter until the UK leaves the EU). If rights have been so abused, the court may reverse the decision.
- Determining whether a public body has exceeded its legal powers (so-called 'ultra vires' cases). If an appeal is upheld, the court may reverse the decision and order compensation where appropriate.
- Determining whether citizens have been treated according to the rule of law and have received equal and fair treatment.
- Determining the correct legal outcome of any disputes that arise between central government and the devolved administrations in Scotland, Wales and Northern Ireland.
- Deciding whether the law has been correctly applied by a lower court in resolving a case. Where the Supreme Court decides the law has *not* been properly applied, it will declare the *true* meaning of the law and is likely to reverse the decision of the lower court.
- Making rulings about how the constitution should operate in the UK, such as in relations between political institutions, political procedures and how powers are to be exercised. The UK lacks a codified constitution so it is ultimately up to the Supreme Court to decide how the constitution should work (at least until parliament makes its own clarification of constitutional law).

Weaknesses of the Supreme Court

Although the UK Supreme Court has developed great strength since 2009, it still has inherent weaknesses that inhibit its ability to protect rights and control the power of government. Among them are these:

- Above all, the court is limited in what it can do by the sovereignty of parliament. However much the judges may believe a law or action by government is unjust or offends human rights, they can do nothing about it if it has been sanctioned by the UK parliament (although the court could set aside laws passed in Scotland because Scotland's parliament is not sovereign). The judges may pass an opinion and put pressure on government, but they do not have the legal authority to cancel a law or reverse a decision.
- Similarly, the court does not have a codified and entrenched constitution to support its deliberations and decisions. The UK constitution remains vague in certain respects, so the court must rely on its own interpretations of what the constitution means, and such interpretations may be open to question.
- The court cannot initiate its own reviews. It must wait until a case is brought to it in the form of an appeal from the decision of a lower court. In other words, the court cannot be 'activist' in its approach to problems.

Nevertheless, the strength of the modern court can be illustrated through four cases heard in 2017, outlined below.

Controversial cases in the Supreme Court in 2017

The court's powers and functions described above are extensive and highly significant. It is therefore not surprising that some of the court's decisions are controversial and have wide political implications. To illustrate this, Table 6.1 summarises some Supreme Court appeal cases in 2017, explaining the issues at stake and describing their wider significance:

Table 6.1 Controversial Supreme Court cases, 2017

Name of case	Date	Details	Significance
R (Miller) v Secretary of State for Exiting the European Union	January	On appeal from the High Court. Miller claimed that the government could not trigger Article 50, whereby the UK would leave the EU, without the authorisation of the UK parliament. The court upheld Miller's case and ordered that parliament must pass a resolution.	Some saw it as a victory for parliamentary sovereignty. The government was angered that its authority was being undermined.
R (Kiarie) v Secretary of State for the Home Department	May	The government was deporting foreign criminals without giving them the chance to appeal before they were deported.	The court ruled this was a denial of justice and ordered that such criminals must have the right to appeal. The government saw this as a barrier to its maintaining law and order.
R (A and B — names withheld) v Secretary of State for Health	June	Abortion is largely illegal in Northern Ireland. Some women were therefore travelling to England for a legal abortion. Women A and B had abortions in Manchester and claimed that the NHS should pay the costs of the private abortions in England. Their appeal was rejected.	This demonstrated a principle in relations between UK government (the NHS) and the devolved administration of Northern Ireland. Such devolution issues are unclear and often require clarification.
R (Unison) v Lord Chancellor	July	The government introduced a large increase in the fees to be paid in bringing appeals against unfair dismissal to industrial tribunals. The trade union Unison claimed that the increases stopped people obtaining justice as they could not afford the high fees. The court upheld the appeal and the government agreed to cancel the fee increases.	The court upheld an important principle of justice and forced the government to change its policy.

These cases illustrate both the power of the Supreme Court and the reasons why its powers can be controversial.

In what ways is the court *too* powerful?

When the High Court made its first ruling in the Miller case — that parliament and not government should trigger Article 50 for leaving the EU — the tabloid press expressed huge anger. In a famous headline the *Daily Mail* called the judges 'Enemies of the people', mistakenly believing that the judges were trying to reverse the EU referendum result. The Supreme Court ignored these comments and upheld the ruling in January 2017. By the time of the appeal, emotions had cooled and government ministers were forced to accept the judgment of the court. However, the case did raise questions about who should determine such constitutional issues. Many argued it should be parliament and not judges. In this case, of course, parliamentary power was the issue so the result would have been the same, but there was some questioning over who is sovereign — the people in a referendum, parliament or the elected government, which has a popular mandate. Few would argue that the court would be sovereign in such cases.

The remaining cases shown in Table 6.1 illustrate other problems concerning the court's powers. In summary, these include:

- Fundamentally there is a problem that judges are unelected and therefore unaccountable. It can be argued, therefore, that they should not make decisions of political significance (such as Kiarie in Table 6.1). Such issues should be determined by politicians, who *are* accountable.
- It has also been argued that Supreme Court judges are far from representative of the population, being largely male (even though their president is a woman), elderly, white and from privileged backgrounds. Here again, it could be argued that politicians are more representative than senior judges.
- Some accusations of their excessive power are actually objections to the force of the Human Rights Act. It could be argued that, in some cases, the court uses the Act to thwart the power of government. This is illustrated in the Kiarie and Unison cases shown in Table 6.1, although it could be argued that the judges might have reached the same conclusions *before* the passage of the Human Rights Act under the principles of common law.
- The court's powers with respect to rights can be seen as a serious obstacle to the government's ability to combat terrorism and crime and to maintain national security generally. This has become more acute since the passage of the Human Rights Act.
- When the court is determining constitutional issues, as in the Miller and abortion cases shown above, there is an argument that this should be the preserve of parliament, which is ultimately sovereign.

This is an impressive list of objections to the court's powers. However, the power of the court can also be defended as outlined below.

In what ways might the powers of the court be defended?

The UK does not have a codified constitution and, furthermore, constitutional rules are not entrenched. This places citizens' rights in danger of abuse by government and parliament, and maintains the danger that the executive may claim too much power for itself without any constitutional constraints. The existence of a politically independent court, whose members are committed to maintaining the rule of law, does guarantee a safeguard for our rights and a barrier to government claiming too much power. The main advantages of such a court include the following:

- Judges are politically independent.
- Judges are legally trained and have vast legal experience, so they understand the principles of law and the rule of law.
- The Supreme Court has been granted considerable authority since the 2005 Constitutional Reform Act. This means it can be a powerful counterbalance to executive power.

International comparisons

In assessing the relative strength of the UK Supreme Court it is worth making some international comparisons. Though we may think the Supreme Court is powerful, it is, in fact, much less powerful than most of its counterparts in the democratic world. Constitutional courts in other countries, such as the US Supreme Court and the French Constitutional Council, are considerably more significant.

Courts in systems where there is a codified constitution have the power to determine constitutional issues and may set aside laws that are deemed to be 'unconstitutional'. The parliaments in these countries are not sovereign, but, instead, are subject to rulings by the constitutional court.

In France and the USA, for example, there is no questioning of the rights of the constitutional court to control governmental power and to protect citizens' rights. Having said that, it can also be argued that they are *too* powerful. Some commentators argue that the balance of power between the UK Supreme Court and the UK parliament is a healthy feature, allowing government to govern effectively through the sovereignty of parliament, but also enjoying a robust defence of our rights.

Conclusion

It may well be that the Supreme Court will be thrust into the political limelight in the years to come as the UK leaves the EU. There are many unanswered questions about issues such as the status of economic and social rights, who should adjudicate in future trade disputes and what UK laws may replace current EU laws. In other words, some of the functions currently performed by the European Court of Justice may be taken over by the UK Supreme Court. Apart from anything else, it may find itself overwhelmed with work!

The appropriate final conclusion to this question is to consider the important doctrine of the independence of the judiciary. The creation of the Supreme Court marked a big step towards genuine judicial independence.

The key to this change lies with the improved status of the Supreme Court. In other words, asking whether the Supreme Court is too powerful is the wrong question. The right question perhaps should be: how independent is the court and the rest of the judiciary?

Exam focus

To consolidate your knowledge of this chapter, answer the following questions:

1 Explain the main functions of the Supreme Court.
2 Explain the main limitations of the Supreme Court.
3 To what extent can the Supreme Court protect rights in the UK?
4 To what extent can the Supreme Court control the power of government in the UK?
5 Why have there been criticisms of the actions of judges in the UK in recent years?

Chapter 7

Pressure groups: three contemporary case studies

Exam success

The up-to-date facts, examples and arguments in this chapter will help you to produce good-quality answers in your AS and A-level tests in the following areas of the specifications:

Edexcel	AQA
1.1 Democracy and participation	3.1.2.4 Pressure groups

Context

The activities of pressure groups have never been as important as they are today. This is for a number of reasons which include the following:

- The lack of a decisive government with a solid parliamentary majority since 2010 has made politicians more susceptible to external pressure. All parties are fighting hard for votes and so need the support of important pressure groups.
- The Brexit process has brought many groups into the political arena, hoping to gain favourable circumstances as a result of the negotiations going on with the EU.
- The importance of the internet and social media as channels of information and influence have thrust many new groups into the political arena.
- The access points available for pressure have grown with the increased level of devolution and the emergence of city and regional mayors with considerable powers and budgets. On the other hand, after the UK leaves the EU, insider groups in particular will find it is possible to be more focused in their efforts, with many powers being returned to the UK.

This chapter examines what we can learn from the experience of three very different types of pressure group.

The Fawcett Society

Background

The society is named after Millicent Fawcett (1847–1929), who was a prominent suffragist. Unlike the suffragettes, Fawcett and the suffragists insisted that the methods used to campaign for women's votes should be peaceful. It was established in 1866 when Millicent Fawcett herself started a petition for women's suffrage. However, the society only gained major prominence in modern times when the feminist movement blossomed in the 1970s. It can be described as both a **promotional** group (equal rights etc.) and a **sectional** group (representing women).

Aims

The stated aims of the Fawcett Society are to:

- change public attitudes towards the role and status of women in society
- secure equal pay for women
- promote more women into positions of political, economic, social and cultural power
- defend the rights of women

Methods

The principal methods used by the society include:

- conducting research into discrimination against, and negative attitudes towards, women, producing reports as a result of such research and using them to educate and to campaign for women's rights
- lobbying politicians and other decision-makers and organising meetings and conferences in order to promote action
- conducting public campaigns to publicise the problems faced by women in modern society

Membership

In 2017 the society claimed only 3,000 members but has a number of 'celebrities' who support it actively, including comedians Bill Bailey and Josie Long, Radio 4 *Woman's Hour* presenter Jenni Murray, novelist Kate Mosse and actor Sir Patrick Stewart. It is currently conducting a drive to raise its profile and increase its membership. However, it concentrates on gaining the help of high-profile supporters and forging close links with politicians.

Prominent campaigns

Among its current campaigns are to:

- persuade government and decision-makers to close the persistent pay gap between men and women. Despite equal pay legislation, women still tend to be paid less than men
- promote the establishment of more women in important political roles and positions at local, regional and national levels
- ensure that the principal of equal pay and treatment of women will be preserved after Brexit
- strengthen legislation and police action against domestic violence
- publicise the persistence of sexist attitudes in various institutions and in society in general

Assessment

It is difficult to assess the impact of the society. However, there is little doubt that it influenced Labour governments after 1997 and was an influence behind Harriet Harman's Equality Act of 2000. It is an ideal example of an 'insider' group, with good access to decision-makers, that engages in lobbying and persuasion rather than direct action through mass membership. It is likely to have more influence on Labour and 'liberal' Conservatives governments (such as under David Cameron 2010–16) than on the current Conservative Party leadership. The society received

a boost in September 2017 when it was announced that a new statue of Millicent Fawcett is to be erected in Parliament Square.

Frack Off

Background

There is no formal date for the foundation of this pressure group, but it came into existence at about the time when the government began to offer licences to oil companies to begin testing for suitable fracking sites after 2010.

Fracking is a process of extracting oil and gas deposits from underground shale by pumping liquid at high pressure into the shale, causing it to fracture and release the deposits. It is highly controversial for environmentalists, as many scientists believe it destabilises the ground and can provoke earthquakes and tremors, causing great damage at the surface. It may also despoil areas of natural beauty and disturb wildlife.

Frack Off is not a single group but more a federation of many local activist groups. Essentially it operates as a 'clearing house' and information system for all those concerned about fracking. It is therefore very much part of the modern social media age. It is certainly a **promotional** group, though it can also be described as sectional in that it represents local environmental interests.

Aims

Frack Off has one main aim, which is to stop both experimental and operational fracking in the UK. It also opposes a variety of other forms of exploration for oil and gas that are considered environmentally dangerous. It should also be seen as part of the wider opposition to fossil fuel burning in the interests of preventing climate change. In this sense the anti-fracking movement is supported by such groups as Friends of the Earth and Greenpeace.

Methods

The movement concentrates on putting pressure on government not to award licences for fracking. These licences can be granted at local, devolved and national level, so the group operates at all levels. It uses a variety of methods to apply this pressure, but the main three are:

- Organising protests on the ground, involving disruption to fracking operations. These protests often involve occupying premises and disrupting the work of fracking companies. Protests often involve stunts, designed to attract maximum publicity. In 2011, protesters scaled Blackpool Tower to unfurl an anti-fracking banner.
- Publicising reports and information that suggest fracking is an undesirable activity. There is, for example, an online newsletter. This involves a certain amount of direct lobbying of decision-makers at local, regional and national level.
- Coordinating the work of local groups to ensure maximum coverage. This largely involves the use of the internet in general and social media in particular. In this way demonstrations can be organised quickly and without too much forewarning for the authorities.

Membership

Frack Off does not have a formal membership so it is impossible to assess its size. It is also a broad movement covering many local organisations and protest groups. However, it is certainly widespread as a movement and probably has followers who can be numbered in tens, possibly hundreds, of thousands.

Prominent campaigns

The work of the movement is largely directed against Cuadrilla, the most prominent fracking company operating in the UK. The most successful action has been to persuade local authorities, particularly in Lancashire and Cheshire, to refuse permission for exploration work. However, companies have successfully appealed to national government to overturn such decisions.

The movement achieved a major victory in October 2017 when the Scottish parliament voted to ban fracking altogether in Scotland. This was the result of a sustained campaign of civil disobedience and lobbying. Of course, the movement was aided by the fact that three parties in Scotland — the SNP, Labour and the Liberal Democrats — opposed fracking. This success echoed a smaller victory already won in Northern Ireland in 2015 when anti-fracking groups persuaded Rathlin Energy to cease operations in Northern Ireland in the face of mass protests. It has also delayed the progress of fracking exploration in Lancashire, though it has been unable to stop it completely.

Assessment

This is an excellent example of a pressure group that can also be described as a 'social movement'. It exhibits the following characteristics:

- It is a classic 'outsider' pressure group as it has few direct links with government.
- It is a mass membership ('follower' is a better term than member) group.
- It is an example of a group that relies almost exclusively on social media and the internet to organise its activities.
- Its relatively limited success is the result of the fact that its aims are at odds with government policy, which is to encourage fracking. This does not, however, apply in Scotland.

UK Finance

Background

UK Finance came into existence in September 2017. It is the amalgamation of a number of existing groups that represented various sections of the financial establishment in the UK. Among these groups were the British Bankers' Association (BBA), the Council of Mortgage Lenders, the Asset Based Finance Association (ABFA) and the UK Card Association. The idea behind the amalgamation is to concentrate influence in one organisation, especially in view of the Brexit process, which is likely to affect financial institutions a great deal. It is very much a **sectional** pressure group.

Aims

The aims of the new group include ensuring that the Brexit agreement currently being negotiated creates the best possible outcome for the finance sector in the UK. It will also seek to influence government policies in areas that include:

- banking and financial regulation in general
- taxation issues
- fraud and identity theft
- credit and mortgage controls
- government financial policy in general
- issues relating to competition in the finance sector
- policies to ensure that London remains a major world financial centre
- future trade deals with the EU and outside the EU

Methods

UK Finance promises to be the ultimate insider pressure group. It will have close links with the government and the Treasury in particular. The methods it will use will include:

- gathering important financial data and feeding this to financial decision-makers in government
- lobbying ministers, officials and MPs
- securing places on government policy-making committees
- providing evidence to parliamentary committees
- ensuring media coverage of the concerns of its members

Membership

At its inauguration, UK Finance claimed to have 300 companies as members. This may not seem many, but most of the members are very large, wealthy organisations, including all the big banks and asset-management companies.

Prominent campaigns

It is too early to assess which campaigns are going to become prominent. However, Brexit is the most important example of its work. In general the organisations represented by UK Finance wish to protect the interests of financial institutions as the UK leaves the EU. However, the financial sector will also be seeking sympathetic treatment by government in terms of taxation and regulation.

Assessment

UK Finance will undoubtedly become one of the most influential pressure groups in the UK. This is for a number of reasons:

- The financial sector in the UK accounts for a large amount of employment and so holds a strategic position in society.
- Similarly, financial services account for a large proportion of UK exports to the rest of the world.
- Financial institutions pay large amounts of tax and this gives them leverage with government.

- The leadership of the group will have strong links with members of the government and the civil service. There has been a good deal of movement of senior managers between the private and public sectors in both directions. In this sense, it is a strong insider group.
- The cooperation of banks and other financial institutions is important for the implementation of government financial policy.
- The institutional members of UK Finance can provide government with vital financial information for the purposes of policy-making.

All these factors suggest that this group is an example of elitism. This is because a huge amount of influence and political resources are concentrated in the hands of a relatively small group of companies and their managers.

Exam focus

To consolidate your knowledge of this chapter, answer the following questions:

1 Using examples, distinguish between sectional (interest) groups and promotional (cause) groups.
2 Using examples, distinguish between insider and outsider pressure groups.
3 In relation to pressure groups, distinguish between pluralism and elitism.
4 How does the status of a pressure group influence its methods?
5 Using examples, to what extent do pressure groups enhance pluralist democracy?

Conclusion

We can use these three case studies to illustrate the characteristics, methods, and relative success or lack of success, of groups. These are summarised in Table 7.1.

Table 7.1 Three pressure groups assessed

Group	Similar groups	Status/ classification	Main method(s)	Main factors in success	Factors in lack of success	Key features
Fawcett Society	• Liberty • Stonewall	• Insider • Promotional and sectional	• Lobbying decision-makers	• Close links with government • Celebrity support • Mostly sympathetic government	• Small membership • Low public profile	• Growing in importance
Frack Off	• Plane Stupid • Stop HS2	• Outsider • Promotional	• Direct action • Internet and social media campaigns • Publicity stunts	• Large mass membership • Successful use of modern media	• Unsympathetic governments • Powerful vested interests (energy companies)	• Good example of pluralist democracy
UK Finance	• Confederation of British Industry • Institute of Directors	• Insider • Sectional	• Lobbying decision-makers	• Insider links with government • Strategic position in society	• Left-wing governments will be unsympathetic	• Good example of elitism

Chapter 8

Constitution: time for a British Bill of Rights?

Context

For some time past the Conservative Party has added to its policy aspirations the introduction of a British Bill of Rights, either to replace or to stand alongside the European Convention on Human Rights (ECHR). Since 2010, however, it has been unable to introduce such a measure, largely because it has not enjoyed a working majority in parliament. All the other parties (with the exception of UKIP) oppose such a measure so there has been little or no chance of securing a majority of support for it. Nevertheless, it remains Conservative policy. This chapter examines what such a Bill of Rights would entail and examines the prospects for its future introduction.

How are rights currently protected in the UK?

One of the main arguments for introducing a British Bill of Rights is that the current position regarding rights protection in the UK is somewhat confused, not least because there are a number of different sources of rights in the UK. This is in marked contrast to many other democracies that have their own Bill of Rights which is entrenched in their constitution. In other words, countries with codified constitutions, such as the USA, Germany or France, have a single source of individual and collective rights.

The unusual situation in the UK is that there are several sources. These are:

- **Common law**. This is law that has existed for many years and has been confirmed by judges in what are known as judicial precedents whenever the nature of rights has come into question during court cases. It is unwritten law in the sense that parliament has not passed any legislation relating to such rights. Common law rights typically relate to the rules of a 'fair trial', the rights of husbands and wives in relation to each other, and rights of inheritance.

- **Equity**. This is similar to common law and is best described as common conceptions of 'fairness'. It is typically used to establish and confirm rights in relation to commercial practices and trading in general.
- **Statute law**. From time to time the UK parliament is required to clarify and develop rights by passing statutes. These have the immediate force of law and must be enforced by the courts. Typical examples are various Habeas Corpus Acts, which forbid any authority from holding people suspected of a crime for any significant length of time without bringing them to trial, or the Equality Act of 2010 which forbids discrimination against any individual or group and so guarantees rights against unfair treatment.
- **European Union law**. These regulations normally relate to people's economic and social rights, such as the right to fair employment practices and the right to fair treatment in welfare provision and pensions.
- **The European Convention on Human Rights (ECHR)**. This is, effectively, a Bill of Rights enforceable in the 47 members of the Council of Europe (not to be confused with the European Union). It describes a wide range of rights to be enjoyed by citizens of the member states. In most member countries it has the full force of law, but in the UK it does not have to be enforced by parliament. This is because the UK parliament remains sovereign. In other words, the UK parliament has the power to pass laws that contravene the ECHR. This apparent contradiction is one of the reasons why a British Bill of Rights is an attractive proposition.

What are the arguments against the ECHR?

There is one overriding objection to the ECHR commonly expressed in the UK, mainly among conservatives. This is that it is outside the control of the UK. In other words, there is the same objection as there has been to the UK's membership of the EU. However, there are also detailed objections to some aspects of the Convention. These problems include the following:

- The ECHR contains a section guaranteeing 'family life' as a right. This has caused problems in the UK when attempts have been made to deport foreign criminals but these have been thwarted because they have established some sort of family in the UK and deportation would break up that family.
- The right to freedom of expression has seriously interfered with the attempts of government to prevent hate and terrorist propaganda from being published on the internet.
- The right to a speedy trial and to be free from imprisonment without trial inhibits the security services in their attempts to prevent terrorist activity.
- The privacy provisions of the Convention make it difficult for the police and security services to monitor the communications and movements of suspected terrorists and criminals.

These and other problems have frustrated both Conservative and Labour governments. The introduction of a British Bill of Rights, many argue, would be an opportunity to remove these difficulties by amending the terms to deal with the situations described above.

What difference would a British Bill of Rights make?

The replacement of the ECHR with a British Bill would have a number of political and judicial consequences. The situation with the ECHR includes these principles:

- The terms of the ECHR are determined by external bodies — the Council of Europe and the European Court of Human Rights. Critics say this defies democratic principles.
- The UK has only a minor degree of influence over the terms of the ECHR.
- This mean that parliament and government in the UK cannot alter the terms of the ECHR for their own political purposes.
- Critics say this severely curtails the power of UK political institutions.
- Supporters say this is an essential safeguard for rights protection in the UK.

In contrast, the situation with a British Bill of Rights would include these principles:

- The terms of the British Bill would be controlled by the UK parliament.
- This would mean that government and parliament could adjust the Bill to take current circumstances (such as terrorist threat or social media problems) into account.
- Supporters argue this would be more democratic than arrangements with the ECHR.
- Critics argue that rights would then be vulnerable in the face of political expediency.

The case for a British Bill of Rights

Option 1: Adding to the ECHR

This option has been supported at various times by liberals, conservatives and members of the Labour Party. Adding to the ECHR implies two consequences:

1 The ECHR could be brought more up-to-date to take account of modern developments, such as those thrown up by international terrorism and social media. It also needs to be updated to take account of modern employment practices (zero hours employment, Uber taxis etc.) and internet consumer practices.

2 In order to deal with threats from international terrorism or hate crimes and other developments, some exceptions need to be added, whereby some rights could be temporarily set aside in the interests of security etc.

We might call this a British Bill of Rights, but it could also be described as the 'ECHR Plus'. As things stand, however, the political circumstances will not allow such a solution to take hold. To be successful, such a proposal would require a government with the political will to carry through the measure and a working parliamentary majority. Neither of these is in sight as things stand.

Option 2: Parallel bills

This proposal has been widely criticised for the judicial problems it would throw up. If there were two codified sets of rights operating together, judges would have difficulty deciding which one they should enforce if there were a conflict between the two.

A solution to this problem would be to establish that, in any conflict between the ECHR and a British Bill of Rights, the latter should prevail. This would beg the question: what would be the point of the ECHR if a British Bill were superior? The answer to this objection is that the ECHR would be advisory and judges would follow it in appropriate cases, while the British Bill would be obligatory.

This remains the most likely development. It would be a compromise, allowing liberals to be satisfied that rights would still be robustly protected, while conservatives would be satisfied that the UK government and UK judges would retain some control over how rights were enforced.

Option 3: Replacing the ECHR

This might be described as the 'nuclear' option and it is supported largely by right wingers in the Conservative Party and by UKIP. The arguments for a British Bill of Rights and a clean break from the ECHR include:

- UK rights would be controlled by UK political institutions.
- Rights in the UK would be designed to suit the specific circumstances in the UK.
- UK rights would be enforced only by UK judges.
- There would be no appeal to an appeal court of foreign judges, as is the case with the ECHR.

The problem with this option is that the Conservative Party stands virtually alone in supporting the measure. In other words, there is little chance of a consensus being created. Only a Conservative government with a large parliamentary majority would have a realistic chance of replacing the ECHR completely with a British Bill of Rights.

Option 4: A codified and entrenched constitution

The arguments in favour of a codified constitution for the UK are well known. The key issue here is that an entrenched constitution would be protected against the actions of a temporary government that might try to take too much power for itself and might attempt to reduce the rights of the people in so doing.

Many liberals argue that it is impossible to separate the arguments for entrenched rights from the argument for an entrenched constitution in general. In other words, they argue that a British Bill of Rights would be useless unless the sovereignty of parliament were set aside. As long as parliament remains sovereign, *any* measure to safeguard rights permanently would be futile, liberals insist. This is because a sovereign parliament could amend a Bill of Rights at will and at any time.

So, a full-scale entrenched and codified constitution would contain a Bill of Rights and it would be protected from amendment by parliament. There would be special arrangements (such as a referendum, or a two-thirds majority of parliament) for any amendment to be made. The experience of the USA, where the Bill of Rights section of the constitution has not been amended for 227 years, reinforces this proposal.

Why oppose a British Bill of Rights?

Having reviewed the case for various changes to the UK's arrangements for the protection of rights, we can now summarise the arguments against the introduction of a British Bill of Rights. The arguments include these:

- In principle, it is argued that rights are universal. All citizens of the world are entitled to the same rights, liberal philosophers have insisted, so a 'British' Bill of Rights is a contradiction in terms.
- A British Bill would be inadequate because it could be amended by parliament at any time.
- An external appeal court (the European Court of Human Rights) is more neutral than the UK Supreme Court, which would view rights only from a British perspective.
- A practical argument is that it would be impossible to find widespread agreement about what should be included in a British Bill.

Some of the objections to a British Bill would be removed if it were to be entrenched. However, as this would entail the abolition of the sovereignty of parliament, there is no immediate prospect of this happening.

In September 2017 an e-petition was sponsored by the website 38 Degrees to retain the Human Rights Act and therefore reject a British Bill to replace it. It received over 300,000 signatures. Most of the concern at that time was related to the rights of EU citizens already living in the UK. Without the safeguard of the European Convention, such people and their families would be vulnerable to being repatriated against their will. The right to a family life currently protects them. This illustrates the fact that the debate over a British Bill and the Human Rights Act is very much tied up with the negotiations over Brexit.

Conclusion

The question we must now ask is: what are the prospects for a British Bill of Rights in the future? This is very much dependent on the fortunes of the various parties in the UK. Some facts are known:

- The proposal for a Bill was included in the Conservative Party's 2015 election manifesto and in 2016 the then-justice secretary, Liz Truss, announced that the plan for a Bill would go ahead. However, she added few details and there was no timescale. Strangely, however, she made no proposals for the UK to withdraw from the European Convention on Human Rights, implying that the new Bill would run parallel with the ECHR (option 2 above). It may well be, however, that the Conservatives will, in the future, opt for the 'nuclear' option of abandoning the ECHR altogether and replacing it with a British Bill (option 3 above).
- Before the 2017 election campaign, the Conservative manifesto committed the UK to the ECHR for 5 years at least, in order to 'avoid any confusion while Brexit is being negotiated'. Once Brexit was completed, however, it was likely that the Conservatives would revive interest in either the replacement of the ECHR (option 3 above) or parallel sets of codified right.

When the Conservatives failed to win a majority, it seemed that prospects for a British Bill of Rights had receded into the distance.

■ The Human Rights Act of 1998, which brought the ECHR into UK law, was introduced by the Labour Party. It is therefore no surprise to learn that Labour does not wish to see it replaced by a British Bill of Rights. However, the shadow justice secretary, Keir Starmer, does support the idea of incorporating the EU Charter of Human Rights into UK law after Brexit. The EU Charter includes all the terms of the ECHR but has certain additions, including the right to dignity in work, bioethics, data protection and the right to freedom of information. This would therefore constitute option 1 above — adding to the ECHR. On Brexit, the Conservatives and their partners, the DUP, propose that the EU Charter will be set aside.

■ The Liberal Democrats support Starmer's policy, but hope to take things further in the future. The party supports the long-term aspiration of a codified constitution for the UK (option 4 above). If the UK were to introduce such a codified and entrenched constitution it would effectively contain a Bill of Rights which would guarantee rights. This would replace the ECHR, though it would almost certainly contain all the rights in the ECHR and more besides. The idea of a codified constitution is also supported by the major reform pressure groups, Unlock Democracy and Liberty.

Exam focus

To consolidate your knowledge of this chapter, answer the following questions:

1 What is meant by the term 'Bill of Rights'?
2 Why do most conservatives favour the introduction of a British Bill of Rights?
3 Explain the main *judicial* objections to a British Bill of Rights.
4 Explain the main *political* objections to a British Bill of Rights.
5 How might a British Bill of Rights differ from the European Convention on Human Rights?

Chapter 9

European Union: what are the key issues for Brexit?

Exam success

The up-to-date facts, examples and arguments in this chapter will help you to produce good-quality answers in your AS and A-level tests in the following areas of the specifications:

Edexcel	AQA
2.4 Relations between institutions	3.1.2.5 The European Union

Context

The UK is scheduled to leave the European Union in March 2019. Unless something extraordinary happens, Britain's exit will happen, whether or not an agreement about future relations with the EU has been successfully concluded. There are a number of scenarios that may occur in 2019. Among them are these:

- No significant agreements will have been made with the EU. This is known as the 'hardest Brexit' possible. The UK will have no special status in Europe and will be in the same position as any other non-European state. This may also be described as 'no deal'.
- There will be an interim 'transition' period of 2 or more years. The UK would have the same relations with the EU as it has currently, except that it will not technically be a member. The transition period will be used to conclude any future agreement.
- An agreement will have been reached and the UK will no longer be a member either of the European Single Market or of the EU Customs Union, but will have agreed a trading arrangement with the EU to the mutual benefit of both sides. This is a form of 'hard Brexit'.
- There may be a 'soft Brexit' agreed, in which case the UK will leave the EU but will remain a member of the European Single Market and the EU Customs Union. This will mean the UK must obey EU rules, accept the rulings of the European Court of Justice in any trade dispute, and accept a degree of free movement of people and labour.

No deal

It is quite possible that the negotiations between the UK and the EU will fail to reach any sort of conclusion. Should this occur, the UK will simply leave the EU and become an independent state with no special economic relations with any other state. The question then becomes: on what terms will the UK trade with the rest of the world? It is likely that the UK would then join the World Trade Organization (WTO) as a single country.

The WTO has rules which all its members must abide by. In the main this means that they are allowed to charge tariffs (import taxes) on goods at certain agreed rates. Some examples of these rates are: wine 32%; cars 9.8%; wheat 12.8%; gas 4.1%. The UK would not have to charge these rates on imports, but it could not exceed them. It would also mean that countries may charge up to these amounts on UK exports.

There are also a number of other rules concerning how much exports can be subsidised and regulations about the quality and safety of goods. Under these circumstances, the UK would begin to try to negotiate trade agreements with individual countries. Such agreements might include the abolition of tariffs on exports and imports of certain goods. In the long term the UK could also try to negotiate such a trade deal with the EU itself. However, in the absence of such deals the UK would be at the mercy of world markets and barriers put up against its exports. On the other hand, no deal would mean the UK government would have complete freedom of action, notably over immigration.

Table 9.1 summarises some of the advantages and disadvantages of reaching no deal with the EU and falling back on World Trade Organization rules.

Table 9.1 The advantages and disadvantages of no deal with the EU

Advantages	Disadvantages
• The UK would be free to negotiate trade agreements with other countries. • The UK could protect home-based industries by charging tariffs on imports. • The UK would gain complete control over the movement of people and workers in and out of the country. • The UK would be allowed to subsidise home industries.	• UK exports would face tariffs, raising their prices and damaging the economy. • Imports might become expensive if tariffs were levied on them, causing inflation. • The UK would lose its current open access to the enormous European market. • The UK would not be able to rely on the collective power of the EU in negotiating trade deals with other states.

One unknown outcome of no deal would be the extent to which the UK would have an obligation to pay existing financial obligations to the EU (such as contributions to the pension schemes of EU employees). If the UK denied its obligations, it would be subject to a legal challenge under international law.

The transition period

In September 2017 Theresa May announced that the UK would seek a transition period of at least 2 years after leaving the EU in March 2019. Labour quickly agreed with this plan in principle and it has become an accepted likelihood. It is expected that this will give UK industry, finance and commerce time to adjust to the new situation. It will also take the pressure off the exit negotiations.

A few conservative right-wingers, such as Jacob Rees-Mogg, oppose the transition period, seeing it as a way of postponing the execution of the will of the people, but there is a consensus around the plan. Liberal Democrats and others opposed to Brexit even hope that the transition period might last so long that there may be a change of a heart and a fresh referendum might reverse the 2016 decision.

Hard Brexit

As the name suggests, a hard Brexit would be similar to a complete break with the EU. It is supported by those who wish to see the UK benefit to the maximum from Brexit. However, this option is perhaps the least likely to be accepted by the membership of the European Union, so it represents very much an 'act of faith'. The main terms of such an outcome would probably involve the following:

- The UK would no longer be a member of either the European Single Market or the EU Customs Union.
- Nevertheless, the UK would maintain a trading arrangement with the EU that would involve the abolition of tariffs and therefore completely free trade between the UK and the EU.
- The UK, unlike members of the EU, would be free to negotiate special trade deals with countries outside the EU.
- In its dealings with the EU, the UK would no longer be subject to rulings, in any dispute, from the European Court of Justice.
- The UK would maintain complete control over the movement of people and labour into the UK.
- The UK would no longer have any obligations to contribute to the security of the EU in the form of cross-border law enforcement, anti-terrorist measures and military defence. The land border between Northern Ireland and the Republic of Ireland would remain open.
- The UK would pay only the minimum financial compensation for leaving to the EU.

Table 9.2 The advantages and disadvantages of a hard Brexit

Advantages	Disadvantages
• The UK would have minimum financial obligations left over from membership.	• It is likely that members of the EU would not accept this solution and so not allow the UK full access to European markets.
• The UK would have complete control over its borders.	• If the UK loses such access, it may do long-term damage to economic and financial enterprises that rely on European exports.
• The UK would retain access to the European Union market.	
• The UK would be free to make trade deals with other countries.	• The UK would no longer enjoy the benefits of being a member of a large trading bloc in negotiations with other countries.
• The openness of the Northern Ireland–Republic of Ireland border would continue.	
• The UK would no longer be subject to the jurisdiction of the European Court of Justice.	• If the UK restricted immigration there may be long-term shortages of labour in the UK.
	• There would be no mechanism for settling trade disputes with Europe.

Soft Brexit

Again as the name suggests, soft Brexit implies only a partial break with the EU. It is probably the most popular option, both in the UK and in the European Union. The UK would cease to be a member of the EU but would continue to have close trading and other links with the EU. The main features of a soft Brexit would probably include the following:

- The UK would remain a member of the European Single Market, meaning that there would be completely free movement of goods, services, people and finance. There would also be essentially free movement of labour, though the UK might retain some small degree of regulation of the UK labour market.
- The UK would remain a member of the EU Customs Union, meaning there would be no tariffs on goods and services coming into or going out of the UK. However, it would also mean that the UK could not negotiate separate trade deals with other countries.
- In view of its continued membership of the Single Market and the Customs Union, the UK would be subject to rules and regulations. However, as a non-EU member, it would have no control over those regulations – controls which, as a full EU member, it now enjoys.
- There would continue to be cooperation between the UK and the EU on issues such as higher education and research, cross-border law enforcement and defence.
- The UK would have to be subject to the jurisdiction of some form of external law court if there were any trade disputes.
- The UK would have to accept extensive financial obligations on leaving the EU, possibly above £50 billion in total to be paid over up to 20 years.

Table 9.3 The advantages and disadvantages of a soft Brexit

Advantages	Disadvantages
• The UK would continue to have free access to European markets.	• The UK would have minimum control over immigration.
• The UK would continue to enjoy the benefits of various kinds of cross-border cooperation.	• The UK would have to accept trade rules and regulations over which it has no control.
• The UK would enjoy the benefits of being a member of a large trading bloc in trade negotiations with other countries.	• The UK would still be subject to the jurisdiction of an external law court.
• The UK would have a small degree of control over immigration.	• The UK would be required to pay its full financial obligations.

What are the current politics of Brexit?

It is fair to say that the UK political system is completely fragmented as far as Brexit is concerned. There is no consensus between parties and very little *within* parties. Table 9.4 summarises how different elements of the UK political community view the various options for Brexit.

Table 9.4 Brexit and UK politics

Brexit option	Supporters	Issues
No deal	Right-wing conservatives	Any deal with the EU would involve some restrictions on the UK's freedom of action, so it is unacceptable.
Transition	This is official Conservative government and Labour policy.	The transition will ensure that a fully negotiated settlement can be reached. It will also give commerce and industry time to adjust. Opponents of Brexit hope this will last indefinitely.
Hard Brexit	Supported by many leading members of the Conservative Party, including Boris Johnson, Michael Gove and the Brexit negotiators, David Davis and Liam Fox. The left wing of the Labour Party, including Jeremy Corbyn and John McDonnell, currently favours a relatively hard Brexit.	Both Labour and the Conservatives are split between hard and soft Brexiteers. It is still not clear which factions will prevail.
Soft Brexit	Moderate conservative opinion is for a soft Brexit, notably supported by chancellor Philip Hammond. It is also supported by moderate Labour members, the Liberal Democrats, the SNP and DUP.	It is not clear where the prime minister stands. Opinion polls suggest there is a narrow public opinion majority for soft Brexit.

Conclusion

The UK's exit from the European Union is possibly the most critical political issue that has been seen since the country joined in 1973. It is also the most divisive, splitting the whole country and the main political parties. There are many key issues, as described above, but only a limited level of agreement over how to resolve them.

There is also one question which, at this stage, is unanswerable — what kind of exit settlement will prove acceptable to the 27 members of the EU? Any agreement will require the *unanimous* agreement of member states, from little Luxembourg to mighty Germany. In essence, however, it will be the larger countries — Germany, France, Italy, Spain and Poland — that will call the shots. At the end of 2017, there was little indication of what these core countries would be willing to accept.

Exam focus

To consolidate your knowledge of this chapter, answer the following questions:

1 Why is Brexit such a divisive issue in UK politics?
2 Explain the distinction between 'hard' and 'soft' Brexit.
3 Why is Brexit not a 'right-wing' versus 'left-wing' issue?
4 What would the main consequences be of the UK failing to reach an exit agreement with the EU?
5 What are the arguments in favour and against a second referendum on any Brexit agreement reached with the EU?

Chapter 10

Scotland: is nationalism in terminal decline?

Exam success

The up-to-date facts, examples and arguments in this chapter will help you to produce good-quality answers in your AS and A-level tests in the following areas of the specifications:

Edexcel	AQA
2.1 The constitution	3.1.1.5 Devolution

Context

In the autumn of 2017, two national regions voted in referendums for full independence. These were the Kurds in Northern Iraq and the Catalans in northeast Spain. In both cases there was an overwhelming majority in favour of independence, though the Catalonian poll was severely disrupted by the Spanish government. These events rekindled interest in the issue of Scottish independence. Indeed, the Catalan situation is quite similar to Scotland, in that Spain has a devolved political system and Catalonia already enjoys a good deal of autonomy, even boasting its own president.

We do need a word of caution here. There may be, in some cases, a difference between 'nationalism' as such and a desire for complete independence. Many so-called Welsh nationalists, for example, are not seeking independence for Wales, but merely more autonomy and measures to protect the Welsh language and culture. Similarly there are many Scots who consider themselves nationalists but, nevertheless, are hesitant to vote for full independence. Indeed, with the increase in the powers of the Scottish parliament and executive after 2016, many nationalists may now be satisfied that their country has sufficient autonomy from the rest of the UK to maintain its separate identity.

Two years ago the referendums in Catalonia and Kurdistan may well have stirred up the Scots to further action, but since then there have been considerable changes in the political situation over the border so that independence seems to be receding into the distance. This begs the question: is Scottish nationalism in decline? This chapter examines the evidence.

The changing fortunes of the Scottish National Party (SNP)

We can trace the fortunes of the SNP in two main ways. The first is to see how many votes and seats have been won by the SNP in elections to the Scottish parliament. These are shown in Table 10.1. The second is to see how many votes and seats the SNP has won at the Westminster parliament in UK general elections. These are shown in Table 10.2.

Table 10.1 Votes and seats won by the SNP in the Scottish parliament

Date	Votes won (%)	Seats won
1999	28.7	35
2003	23.7	27
2007	32.9	47
2011	45.4	69
2016	46.5	63

Table 10.2 Votes and seats won by the SNP in the UK parliament

Date	Votes won (%)	Seats won (in Scotland)
1997	22.1	6
2001	20.1	5
2005	17.7	6
2010	19.9	6
2015	50.0	56
2017	36.9	35

The two pivotal events for the SNP may well prove to have been the 2015 and 2017 general elections. In 2015 the SNP made a huge breakthrough, winning nearly all the seats available in Scotland. Nevertheless, the Conservative Party did secure a majority of 12 seats at Westminster. The SNP *just* failed to hold the balance of power in the UK parliament. Had it done so, the party would have been able to put pressure on the government for more devolution and possibly a second referendum on independence. Similarly, in 2017 the SNP failed narrowly to hold the balance of power. Had the party won seven or eight more seats in Scotland, it would again have been able to exercise leverage against the minority Conservative government.

In the light of these disappointments, the SNP has accepted that there is unlikely to be any more talk of an independence referendum until after the next general election, whenever that may happen, or until after the next Scottish parliamentary election in 2021.

Independence: the changing poll evidence

Table 10.3 Opinion polling, percentage of people responding 'yes' to Scottish independence

Date	Polling organisation		
	YouGov	Survation	Ipsos MORI
December 2014	48	48	–
March 2015	45	45	–
July/August 2015	–	43	53
June/July 2016	40	48	–
March 2017	37	43	47
May/June 2017	39	36	45

Although we can see that there is considerable variation from one polling organisation to another (Ipsos/MORI, for example, seems to estimate consistently higher support for independence than the others), there is a downward trend over the 3 years from 2014 to 2017 in support for independence. However, up to the summer of 2017, support for independence did average at around the actual result of the 2014 referendum, when 45% of the electorate voted for a break from the UK. These data should be viewed in the context that in the 1970s, 1980s and 1990s polls indicated that support for independence typically reached barely 10%.

Further conflicting evidence was revealed by the annual Scottish Social Attitudes survey (**www.ssa.natcen.ac.uk**) in March 2017. This survey found that support for independence was at its highest-ever level in the survey, with 46% favouring a clean break from the UK. This compared with 42% supporting devolution arrangements, and only 8% favouring no devolution at all and the abolition of the Scottish parliament.

Nevertheless, the same survey revealed that a growing number of Scots now feel sceptical about the EU, with 25% wanting the UK to leave and 42% wanting the powers of the EU to be significantly reduced. This implies that only about one-third of Scots wish to remain in the EU in its present form. Since one of the main drivers of Scottish nationalism has been a desire for Scotland to remain in the EU, this suggests that the tide may be turning.

A counter-argument from the survey, however, suggests that Scottish nationalism and a desire for independence is set to grow — 72% of 16–24-year-olds who were surveyed (bear in mind that, in Scotland, 16–17-year-olds are allowed to vote in an independence referendum) still support independence, whereas in the over-65 group independence is supported by only 26%. So, support for the Union may, literally, be dying out and support for independence growing.

Scottish independence timeline

2011	The SNP wins 69 seats in the Scottish parliament with a 45% share of the vote.
2012	UK Prime Minister David Cameron and Scottish First Minister Alex Salmond sign an agreement to hold a referendum on Scottish independence.
2013	The Scottish Parliament votes to sanction a Scottish independence vote.
2014	The Scottish referendum. The Scots vote 'no' to independence by 55–45%.
2015	The SNP wins 50% of the Scottish vote and 59 Westminster seats in the general election.
2016 (March)	The Scotland Act grants much increased devolution powers, including over some direct taxes, to the country.
2016 (June)	The UK votes to leave the EU but a large majority of Scots vote to remain in the EU.

2017 (March)	The Scottish parliament votes in favour of a second referendum on Scottish independence. The Scottish first minister and leader of the SNP, Nicola Sturgeon, argues this is justified as the 'circumstances' in Scotland have changed since the previous referendum as the UK has voted to leave the EU against Scotland's will.
2017 (June)	In the general election the SNP loses 21 seats and 12% of its share of the vote.
2017 (June)	Nicola Sturgeon announces that there will be no second independence referendum until after the UK's Brexit talks have been concluded.

Admitting that Scotland was not ready for a second referendum on independence, Nicola Sturgeon set out her party's position in a speech to the Scottish parliament on 24 June 2017. She said:

> At the end of this period of negotiation with the EU — likely to be around next autumn [of 2018] — when the terms of Brexit will be clearer, we will come back to parliament to set out our judgement on the best way forward at that time, including our view on the precise timescale for offering people a choice over the country's future.

By September 2017, however, Ms Sturgeon was putting the idea of a referendum even more on to the backburner. In a television interview, she said:

> ...I said before recess that I will not consider any further the question of a second referendum at this stage... I'm saying, OK, people are not ready to decide we will do that, so we have to come back when things are clearer and decide whether we want to do it and in what timescale.

Does devolution mean that full independence is unnecessary?

Devolution was granted to Scotland in 1998 when a Scottish parliament and executive were established with wide powers over such services as health, education, policing, criminal and civil law, transport and agriculture. When the Scottish independence referendum campaign was underway in 2014, UK politicians became alarmed when opinion polls suggested there was a fair chance that Scotland might vote for independence.

Leading members of the coalition government of the day, as well as senior Labour Party figures, formally agreed that it was necessary to offer the Scots even more devolved powers in an effort to head off the demands for full independence. Even though the Scots voted against full independence, it was clear that the nationalist tide was running very high and that this needed to be recognised. True to their word, therefore, plans were laid for more devolution (sometimes called 'devo-max'). The Conservative government that won a narrow victory in the

2015 general election pledged to honour these commitments. As a result the Scotland Act was passed in March 2016. The main terms of the Act were as follows:

- The Scottish government was given powers to change the political structure in Scotland, provided any changes were approved by a two-thirds majority of the Scottish parliament. This included the power to change the electoral system.
- The Scottish government was given powers over a range of welfare benefits, including housing, disability and carers' benefits and allowances. Power over universal credit was also devolved.
- The power to set income tax rates and allowances was transferred to the Scottish government.
- The Scottish government was given control of the revenues from several minor taxes including air passenger duty.
- The devolved government was also given the power to regulate telecommunications in the country.
- The Scottish government was granted control over half the total receipts from VAT raised in Scotland (though the Scottish government was not allowed to change the rate of VAT).

These changes represented a large transfer of powers from London to Edinburgh. Powers over welfare and taxation were the most eye-catching changes. By giving the Scottish government increased control over its own finances, the country gained an impressive degree of autonomy.

Increased devolution may well be part of the reason why Scottish nationalism is waning. It has also resulted in some increased support for the Conservative Party, which was responsible for the extension of devolution. The Scots seem more than willing to reward any party that is willing to recognise their demands for more autonomy.

Conclusion

In our conclusion we can usefully summarise the arguments supporting the idea that Scottish nationalism and a desire for independence is holding firm, against the counter-argument that it is, in fact, waning. This is shown in Table 10.4.

Table 10.4 Is Scottish nationalism and the desire for independence firm or is it declining?

Evidence of nationalism standing firm	Evidence that it is declining
Opinion polling suggests that support for independence is still just below 50% despite a small recent fall.	Electoral support for the SNP, both at Westminster elections and in Scotland, is falling.
Younger age groups support independence in much larger numbers than oppose it. This means that overall opinion is likely to swing towards independence as time passes.	The Scots may be becoming more disillusioned with the EU and so may be willing to remain in the UK and leave the EU.

Evidence of nationalism standing firm	Evidence that it is declining
Despite some setbacks, the SNP remains the dominant party in Scotland.	The most recent opinion polling suggests some decline in support for independence.
Many Scots may be waiting for the outcome of Brexit negotiations. If the talks go badly many may well return to supporting independence.	Even Nicola Sturgeon seems resigned to the fact that a second referendum on independence is unlikely in the near future as a 'yes' vote would be hard to achieve.

David Torrance summed up the position in the *Guardian* on 10 August 2017 thus:

> Although the first minister still hasn't ruled out a second ballot, the chances of it taking place in the near future are slim, and given that the energy and enthusiasm of the yes movement was predicated on an upcoming referendum, now there isn't one, many activists have lost focus and begun to drift. A few years ago there was a fixed target — 18 September 2014 — now there is little more than a vague and ever-shifting aspiration.

By the end of 2017, Torrance's summation was looking increasingly accurate.

Exam focus

To consolidate your knowledge of this chapter, answer the following questions:

1 Explain why Scottish nationalism became increasingly popular after 2010.
2 Assess the extent to which Scotland is now an autonomous country.
3 Explain the main arguments against Scottish independence.
4 What evidence is there to suggest that Scotland will not achieve independence in the foreseeable future?
5 To what extent does the Scottish National Party dominate Scottish politics?